# SPRINGSTEEN
# No Surrender

# SPRINGSTEEN
# No Surrender
## Kate Lynch

**PROTEUS**
**LONDON/NEW YORK**

PROTEUS BOOKS is an imprint of The Proteus Publishing Group

United States
PROTEUS PUBLISHING COMPANY, Inc.
9 West 57th Street, Suite 4503,
New York NY 10019

Distributed by:
CHERRY LANE BOOKS COMPANY, Inc.
PO Box No 430,
Port Chester, NY 10573

United Kingdom
PROTEUS BOOKS LIMITED
Bremar House, Sale Place,
London W2 1PT

ISBN 0 86276 253 7 (Paperback)
ISBN 0 86276 254 5 (Hardback)

Photocredits: David Corio, Andre Csillag/David Wainwright, Laura Levine, David Redfern, Retna, Rex Features, Ebet Roberts, Joseph Sia, Lawrence Kirsch: Sparrow Photos, Syndication International, Justin Thomas, Etienne Tordoir.

Editor: Kay Rowley

Designed by: Alison Goodhew
Typeset by: Communitype, Wigston, Leicester
Printed in Spain by Cayfosa, Barcelona

Dep. Leg. B. 4531 - 1985

# DEDICATION

*To Sonja and Steve, I love you.*

# ACKNOWLEDGEMENTS

In roughly chronological order, I'd like to thank some of the people that have helped me with this particular book, and some that have been of much more general assistance. First I'd like to thank Alan Horing and Jonathon Gregg, K. J. Holmes, Tina Medders and Steve Mereu for the research end of it. Likewise, I've gotten a variety of assistance and inspiration from Phyllis 'Super Mom' Tornetta and her son Paul, the Super Fan, as well as Diane Levitt, Mike Brecher and Kay Rowley of Proteus. Thanks as usual go to Norman and Natalie, and this time to Kaz and Andy S. There are also several writers on the subject whom I'd like to thank, particularly Dave Marsh and Peter Gambaccini for their books, as well as periodical writers of whom Peter Knoebler, Robert Hillburn, Kit Rachlis, Paul Nelson, Fred Schuers, Debby Miller, Chet Flippo, Robert Christgau and A Pine are just a few. There is also Jon Landau who was once best known for his writing, as well as Barbara Carr and Denise Sileci who were much nicer to me than they had to be. The same goes for Marilyn Laverty of CBS. Special thanks is due to Charles 'I'm A Rocker' Cross, Editor of Backstreets, and to Ken Viola, whose help arrived at the midnight hour.

In the category of both general and particular support I'd like to publicly thank my family for everything they know they've done. So here's love to Bill, Mitz, Bill my brother, Tricia (and Stefano), Sean, Kevin, Mike and especially to Stephen and Maryann who may now understand why we ended up taking our vacation on the Shore last summer. I'd also like to thank some people who didn't previously know that they were my models for this project; Frank Floyd, Uncle Mike and Mr. Robert Frane who's no longer here to read this but remains a model nonetheless. I'd also like to thank Anne Hogg for all her uncredited help over the years, and likewise to George (Jorge) Pardo who's been known to help me more than he helps himself. Thanks also to the Mereu's and their 'Brother'.

Last, but foremost, I'd like to thank Bruce Springsteen both for what he's done and for what I've inadvertently learned in studying him. I feel personally indebted and I know the same holds true for nearly all of his fans, from whom I've *also* learned quite a bit. So my last acknowledgement goes to two fans, Leonard Cetrangoto and William J. Macchi of Jersey City, N.J., who request that you hold the applause.

I could go on and on with this, but for all the great people who haven't gotten a mention, I just hope that I can do another seventy books and get everybody's name in.

# CONT

M.U.S.E., M.S.G., N.Y.C.

# ENTS

# INTRODUCTION

I've got *Born In The U.S.A.* cranked up so loud that the typewriter is just a rhythm instrument and my sense of reason is gone. This is one way to do things when you've just written an entire book and are forced to admit that you're not nearly equal to your subject. The same is true of Springsteen's music and the fact that the more I listen to this album, the more amazed I am at its brilliance, though I don't know if I brought the same quality to its analysis. My apologies for all this and more.

I had several subjects in mind when I first sat down to write this, and one was Springsteen as The Artist as Hero. I think I've called him both an artist and a hero but perhaps haven't made the point that he's a hero on account of his art, and has become one through it. This is also tied up with where and when and how he's exercising his creative powers (i.e., through rock 'n' roll in the U.S.A. in the latter half of the twentieth century) and the fact that he is that rare person who's making high art in the context of popular (mass) culture. I have really only been able to scratch the surface of how he's accomplished what he has, ranging from what choices he's made to how he's implemented them and why. Suffice to say that I consider Bruce Springsteen to be the Complete Rock Star because of everything that he does (write, dance, sing, play, act and rock) and the fact that he always does the best he can which just happens to be better than anyone else at the moment. This is to be taken as fact, not opinion, and I'm only sorry that I haven't been able to go into every single detail of his lengthy career. Bruce is Boss, and I've barely talked about his band, who they are and how they do what they do. Likewise, the analysis of the lyrics which occupies a major portion of the book is fairly superficial, and I've barely touched on the dynamic between the words and the music, which anyway needs to be heard to be really appreciated. And for all of the trying to figure out who he is and why, I don't know that I could answer that question about Bruce or anybody else — maybe the questions are bigger than me and Springsteen and this book. On the other hand, I would highly recommend taking on Bruce Springsteen as a subject of study because what he has to

say is important and there is also a lot of pleasure to be gained from the experience of listening to him speak through music (or perhaps it's actually music speaking through Bruce Springsteen). Either way, it's certainly worth the time spent. There are points in this book in which politics and economy and the state of the world enter the discussion, and it's only right that Springsteen be seen in these terms because he is clearly aware of them. The danger comes when people would like to see or make Bruce or his music a rallying point for their own politics or philosophy (which has been done by people ranging from those on the far left to right-wing nationalists). My point is that above being an entertainer, Springsteen is an artist with the hallmark of both forcing and allowing himself to speak in an honest voice. This makes what he does potentially universal, and though it's not outside of politics, I believe that it's above them. It also means that he's undertaken one of the most difficult tasks that a person can assume.

The record's over now so instead of dancing while I type I find myself getting a little more serious. There were a few points I wanted to make that I either forgot, or which didn't fit into the body of the text, and there were a few questions I was recently asked which I'd like to address.

I had an idea about teaching a course in rock 'n' roll where the final exam would consist of analyzing Bruce Springsteen, because as I make my way backwards (I'm still a student) all the lines about Springsteen embodying the rock 'n' roll tradition while he defines its future, have been seeming more and more valid. The subject of who's influenced Bruce and how is quite popular, but like many other aspects of his life, it's difficult to pin down. There are people that Bruce has mentioned ranging from the obvious Chuck Berry, Elvis, The Beatles, Buddy Holly, Phil Spector, Sam and Dave, The Beach Boys, Bob Dylan etc.. But as he's gone forward, he's also gone backwards and he's an avid listener to things which might not be deduced from his work. In the manner of a shopping list, some of the less obvious major influences would be Paul Jones (original singer from Manfred Mann), John Fogerty of Creedence Clearwater fame ( whose songs Springsteen has been known to cover), The Band (as in Dylan's one time back-up band), Jimi Hendrix and Eric Clapton (for guitar inspiration), The Stones and The Who for their early spirit, Jackie Wilson (for singing), James Brown (for everything) and it really gets to be a never ending list. Especially when Bruce's ear will pick out the one good thing in any song. Needless to say, I've only mentioned rock, soul and R&B which leaves out things like reggae which Bruce listens to but doesn't play, along with the country and folk artists (of whom Hank Williams and Woody Guthrie are the prime examples) and all the blues, gospel, jazz etc., that you know he's checked out and learned from. To this end, you can assume that if something's been on the air (or even if it hasn't), he's heard it. And while everything doesn't get lifted and put straight into a song (contrary to what some critics have charged), this expertise in the history of his field has consistently stood Springsteen in good stead, no matter what he's actually putting on vinyl. To illustrate this point, I'd like to drag out an observation from the Newsweek article of 1975. 'He riffed through his beloved Fifties records — Elvis and Dion — from stacks of albums on the floor which included Gregorian chants, David Bowie and Marvin Gaye.' And that's just the tip of the iceberg.

The same pitfall frequently surfaces regarding literary and film influences and the same for the most part 'he's probably seen everything' seems to hold. (This also goes for TV, from which Bruce has learned most of the classic comedy routines and who knows what else.) So treat any report that Springsteen was reading this book or looking at that film while he worked on an album with caution, because while one work may have been a major influence, chances are there were plenty more besides. He may have talked about seeing *Wise Blood* but does anyone know that he also saw *L'Argent* by Bresson? I would also make the same case for Springsteen's personal life because not only is very little known about his earlier years, but the image of the man is actually a schizo one when you think about it. He's a known loner but he usually has a girlfriend and can be the life of a party and, while he eschews the trappings of fame and wealth in general, he's also able to take advantage of them when he desires. It is the reality of Bruce being conscientiously in touch with real life and people though that enamours him to so many of his fans. I mean this guy who can sell out The Meadowlands will also play down the Turnpike in Asbury Park, so it's no wonder that the Stony Pony is a virtual shrine to Bruce. But the point is, that he wouldn't be doing it unless he wanted to and, aside from the fact that it probably keeps him in touch with the days of playing every dingy bar on the Eastern Seaboard, he really seems to thrive on that up-close energy and exchange with his.

By way of more loose ends (which tie into questions I've been asked), there is a book which some of you may have read called *Born To Run* by Dave Marsh, and I am as indebted as anyone to what still stands as the most comprehensive account of Springsteen that's available. The book has some particularly excellent features like a list of commonly covered-tunes (by Bruce of other people's work) and it goes into a fair amount of detail about business

dealings as well as including some rather thought-provoking and informative tangents. I've had to keep the tangents — and the number of words — to a limit but, for those who've read the other book, (and for those who haven't), there are a couple of points on which I'd take issue. These are not so much with what I imagine is Marsh's perception of Springsteen, as with his presentation. One word that appears fairly often in *Born To Run* is 'instinctive', and though I agree that Bruce seems instinctively on target most of the time, it seems as likely and more important to think of his accomplishments in terms of the conscious struggles that are behind them, rather than making it seem as if Springsteen is a natural and can do no wrong. He may be a perfectionist but he's not perfect. Another minor, but related point, has to do with this image of Springsteen as an unschooled natural genius. While there may be some basis for this, the fact that at an early point in his career he'd only admit to having read *The Godfather* and Scaduto's Dylan biography, ends up being quite misleading. Without mounting a major argument, I'll just relate a comment by a member of the Asbury Jukes who said that when they toured with Bruce, the Jukes bus was the party bus and that Springsteen's looked like a library.

The rest of what I'd like to say is addressed to a group of people that I stood in line with for about eleven hours waiting for tickets to see Bruce at The Meadowlands. What impressed me was that they were interested in *everything* and were so simply eloquent when discussing Bruce's music that I thought of tearing up the whole manuscript. I could answer questions like 'How did he get started in music?' but I couldn't say whether he'd had some tragic love affair at an early age. I was asked if he liked touring and realized that not only did I not speak about the performances very much, I left out the quote about how he likes touring because you just never know what kind of picture is gonna be in the hotel room and so on. I also didn't mention the athletic prowess of Bruce in performance and how he's famous for having a back as hard as a table and an aura of Ben Gay about him when he's finished. He'll also be checking out acoustics in the last row during soundcheck, will be the last one to leave the hall and will still have time for the fans who wait outside for him because he knows what he means to them and respects that. Bruce's relation to his fans is practically a subject for another entire book, but I'd like to tell one story that Bruce told to Dave Marsh and which was retold to me by countless fans. It takes place in Denver where Bruce, after his fashion, goes to see a movie by himself. Some kid recognizes him, talks to him through the whole film and finally says that his Mom would love to meet Bruce and asks him home to dinner. Of course, Springsteen went and loved it. The moral of the story is that the guy is in touch and he cares about his fans and if he wasn't so exceptional in so many other ways, that alone might be enough to ensure the fanatical devotion that's so common among his followers.

I do have a lot more to say that either wouldn't fit into this book or that is a little risky (like my predictions), but I would like to state unequivocally that after spending

several months thinking about and studying Bruce Springsteen, I am definitely in the devotee camp and thus can understand the zealot's urge as well as the frustration that comes with not being able to get others to hear (see and feel) what Bruce's music is about and what it can mean to you. I don't know if this book can serve that purpose, since it seems that direct experience — and the more of it the merrier — is the best solution. But since I have had to leave out so many things, the best suggestion I can make is to get all of the albums, listen to them in order (as Bruce intended), *several* times and it's guaranteed that you'll see and hear things (like everybody else's music) differently. I know I should have said that before you bought the book, but they wouldn't let me put the warning on the cover. (NOTICE: Don't spend your money on this book unless you've got all the albums first.)

Sincerely,

Kate Lynch                                    N.Y.C. 1984

# ONE

# BORN IN THE U.S.A.

There are some popular ideas floating around about 'born artists' and 'God given talents' which persist largely because we don't understand much about ourselves and our capacities. And, while people *are* different and some seem quite special, the real dilemma with this 'born artist' business is that it encourages a view of life that is passive and non-progressive, setting up heroes (in this case artists) as people to be admired while suggesting that they have nothing in common with you or I. Bruce Springsteen has gone a long way towards dispelling these myths, but when people view him as some kind of god or superman, they're bound to miss the real message of his life.

Bruce Springsteen's story is what's usually considered the archetypal tale of the rock hero, as summed up in his favorite line from The Stones' *Street Fighting Man*: 'What can a poor boy do but play for a rock 'n' roll band'. The fact that Bruce was born into a working-class environment in north central New Jersey has certainly had an impact on his art and his life, but perhaps it's more important that he's *chosen* to continue identifying with it. The situation and circumstances that Springsteen was born into link him to millions by virtue of shared experience, but what makes him important — as an artist as well as a person — is that he sought and found more than most people in any situation ever dare. He's said that he 'wanted it all' (and in the process 'lost everything I ever loved or feared'), but what he wanted was not money or power, it was life on a higher level. Just why he set his sights so high and exactly what he's learned in his searches are questions that even Springsteen may not even be able to answer completely. However, there are a few clues in the circumstances of his youth and his reactions to them.

Bruce Springsteen generally chooses to let his music speak for him and many of his familiar childhood tales are recounted in his legendary stage raps. These stories, like his music, incorporate large elements of personal truth but the details shouldn't be taken too literally. They are also valuable since there are few accounts of Springsteen's family background or history from other sources.

For a man with the word 'born' in two album titles you might get the impression that he considers the circumstances of birth to be especially significant. He himself was born on September 23, 1949 in Long Branch, New Jersey and, since his mother hasn't come forth with her version of the story, we'll have to take Bruce's word (from *It's Hard To Be A Saint In The City*) that he was born 'blue and weathered but I burst just like a supernova'. It's doubtful whether much was expected of Bruce Frederick Springsteen's life, but he's struggled against some oppressive odds, and it's had a major impact on his development as an artist. Shortly after the war his father returned from the army and married his mother, Adele Zerilli. They settled in the area Mr. Springsteen had grown up in — north central Jersey, on the fringes of one of the country's largest industrial areas. At the time of Bruce's birth they were living in Freehold (his father's hometown), but due to job-related moves, throughout Bruce's childhood they lived all over an area of New Jersey defined by the coastal towns of Asbury Park, Neptune and Atlantic Highlands, and inland to Freehold where Bruce spent several of his crucial 'growin' up' years. Bruce still lives in the same area in the rather wealthier town of Rumson, because the area not only holds the key to all of his early images and memories, but it's also still home to his old friends. (He also now has a house near L.A. and his family.) When Bruce was a kid the area and its landscape were his entire world, but what it has now come to represent is just as important. Its sights and sounds — everything from strands and swamps to giant Exxon signs, lunar landscapes, refinery towers, auto plants, dynamos and a million roads and highways — continue to inspire him and act as the settings for his songs.

His family life colored his view of the world and most of what makes his vision different seems to stem from his father, Douglas Frederick Springsteen. Bruce once commented that 'there ain't a note I play on stage that can't be traced directly back to my mother and father' and he deals with these relationships in both song and story. The father in his songs is not necessarily his real father, but there is both a personal and universal truth in his father-son songs.

It's clear however that his father's temperament puzzled Bruce and he remains something of an enigma. Almost nothing is known about his life prior to Bruce's birth and when Bruce does speak about him it is usually to conjure up one of a few images. The introduction to The Animals' *It's My Life* is typical of Bruce's portrayal of Douglas Springsteen. 'And my father, he worked a lotta different places, worked in a rug mill for a while, drove a cab for a while, and he was a guard down at the jail for a while. I can remember when he worked down there, he used to come home real pissed off, drunk, sit in the kitchen.

'At night, about nine o'clock, he used to shut off all the lights, every light in the house. And he used to get real pissed off if me or my sister turned any of 'em on. And he'd sit in the kitchen with a six pack and a cigarette... My pop, sometimes he went to bed, sometimes he didn't. Sometimes he got up. Sometimes he didn't.'

The story goes on recounting their fights and how Bruce used to slick his hair 'so he couldn't tell how long it was gettin'' and sneak out of the house. But he'd always get caught, get dragged back in and his father would sit there 'tellin' me, tellin' me, tellin' me. And I could always hear that voice, no matter how long I sat there. But I could never ever see his face.'

Things had changed since the days when his father had been photographed looking, according to Bruce, proud and a lot like John Garfield. Confronted daily with a frustrated, brooding and despairing father, Bruce eventually came to understand that in part it was because he was a product — and casualty — of the 'working life' which most of Bruce's musical characters also live. What Bruce found initially so puzzling in his father eventually furnished him with a key to understanding others in a similar bind, because even if their reactions weren't quite the same, the same forces were working on them. Put simply, you're born, grow up, think you're somebody special, maybe go in the army, get married, get a job, have kids and suddenly your life ain't too great or too special after all.

At about the same time Bruce came into the world, America was revelling in post-WWII prosperity and the American Dream was employed as a sort of mass hypnosis to channel the energy of an entire population. The Dream was sold in a million ways, in magazines, on television, in schools etc., and most people bought it wholesale. But Douglas Springsteen was an exception. On the one hand he was infected by it, but at the same time he also became aware of the hidden tolls. References to the American Dream crop up again and again in Springsteen's lyrics and this one seems particularly relevant to his father's quandry. 'Is a dream a lie if it don't come true, or is it something worse?'

The overall effect was that Douglas Springsteen was somewhat paralyzed by his realizations. He never managed to put on blinders and seek that pie-in-the-sky — home in the suburbs, two new cars in the garage, and don't stop there. He didn't like the kind of work he was 'supposed' to do, yet he took job after job. He worked as a laborer at the race track, in Nestlés and Hershey factories, as a gardener, prison guard, bus driver etc. perpetually working from

'morn to morn'. He didn't completely reject the expectations placed on him — he didn't abandon his family, nor become violent — but, not knowing quite what to do, he kept his frustrations, revelations and bitterness locked up inside. Apparently it tore him up, and seeing this close up had a profound effect on Bruce; he learned to love and respect his father but would never settle for the same fate. He would also later bare these dilemmas in song after song, as in *Adam Raised A Cain* which proclaims that 'Daddy worked his whole life for nothing but the pain/Now he walks these empty rooms, looking for something to blame.' It's a search Bruce has likewise undertaken.

Douglas Springsteen also had a few escape-orientated pastimes that Bruce took up. Bruce has referred to his father as a 'sure money man' on the pool tables (though with Bruce his pinball skill is more widely acknowledged) and he is also a driver. As Bruce described it: 'He liked to get in the car and just drive. He got everybody else in the car too, and made *us* drive. He made us all drive.' Not only did his father's penchant for driving give Bruce early exposure to a car's eye view of his native state, it also exposed him to both the symbolic and actual significance of the car in American society — escape, power, identity. Again with his father as the subject, Bruce got to the heart of some of the major contradictions between The Dream and reality in the song *Used Cars* on the *Nebraska* album. One story Bruce tells about the way the lifestyle you're born into is always bound to seem natural, gives a better picture of their everyday reality. 'My father used to drive around in his car, and it would not go in reverse. Heh. I remember pushing it backward; that was just something you did, you didn't even think it was strange.'

While Douglas Springsteen inadvertently posed questions that would prove to be fertile material for Bruce, his mother and his sisters Ginny and Pam formed the other side of the home equation. Mrs. Springsteen apparently wasn't torn by the same sort of conflicts as her husband and it was mainly due to her energy that the family was able to function. It's only lately that Bruce has made many public comments about her, but everything he's said implies that she was the backbone of the family. As he put it: 'just like Superwoman, she did everything, everywhere, all the time.' On his recent tour he dedicated Clarence Clemons' *Woman's Got The Power* to her, saying that she didn't think it was fair that he only talked about his father on stage. But it's in that same story introducing *It's My Life* that Bruce painted a rather depressing picture of what things were like when he was young. He said, 'My mom, she'd set her hair and she would come downstairs and just turn on the TV and sit in the chair and watch TV till she fell asleep. And she'd get up the next morning and go to work again.' In spite of the trying situation, she was never defeated and managed to help foster a positive self-image in her son. Her family also played a large part in encouraging Bruce's artistic leanings . The Springsteens frequently lived with Mrs. Springsteen's family, and it is from his grandfather Zerilli that Bruce claims to have learned the art of story-telling. Her family was apparently the livelier of the two and this must have helped encourage the clownish side of Bruce's nature.

Bruce's mother is an Italian Catholic (Mr. Springsteen is from an Irish and Dutch background and may also be) and her religion was one tradition she foisted onto Bruce before he had any choice. He was sent to a Catholic grade school (St. Rose of Lima) and was even urged to serve mass; all disastrous experiences. One of Bruce's reactions to such traumas was to adopt a dull mask, remaining as oblivious as possible. It was also one of his earliest strategies for dealing with the nuns and their brand of education. He's mentioned that he spent half of his first thirteen years in a trance, that he was always walking around with this *look* on his face. When he reached the age of twelve he was finally in a position to assert himself, which usually meant rebelling against whatever surrounded him.

'I was like nowhere, on the outs. I had no choice, that's where I was, that's where I got put, that was my place in life all the years I was growing up. I did a lot of running away. And a lot of being brought back. It was always very terrible. It started when I was in sixth grade.'

Prior to the age of twelve Bruce took in a lot of impressions but had no real outlet or sense of his own possibilities. What school and Catholicism inadvertently did was to hone his instinct for questioning and rebellion, and it also made him aware of how he might escape from where he 'got put'. He talks about becoming 'the crazy guy in class' just to maintain some sense of humanity and humor in the deadening school environment, but 'I didn't even make it to class clown, I had nowhere near that amount of notoriety. I didn't have, like, the flair to be a complete jerk. It was like I didn't exist; it was the wall then me.' He was however notorious enough to be handed some classic punishments like being stuffed in a trashcan and told that's where he belonged, but as he claims in *Growin' Up*, he came out with his 'soul untouched'. Furthermore, he turned these negative lessons into a hallmark of his own philosophy, saying that 'I will never put someone in the position of being humiliated. It happened to me for far too long.'

One of the mysteries of Springsteen's character is how such a self-confessed introvert could ever become such a transcendent entertainer. As a young kid he developed some discipline through baseball, which he practised for hours each day, though he modestly claims that he was never any good. Music, though, allowed him personal expression and creativity and he was later able to say with no exaggeration that 'music saved me'.

Prior to discovering music, Bruce was discontented and in the same situation that one cynical reporter described as typical of New Jersey high school students as late as 1984. He said 'they are tracking themselves into the same kind of lives and jobs their parents have'. However, thanks to his father, Bruce was able to see where things would lead and consciously began to seek a way out.

He got his first real glimpse of freedom the night Elvis Presley appeared on the Ed Sullivan show. His reaction was: 'Man, when I was nine I couldn't imagine anyone *not* wanting to be Elvis Presley.' From a later vantage point, Bruce saw the larger picture and remarked about Elvis that

Bruce revisits the site of the factory where his father used to work, only to find it closed.

'There ain't no more. Everything starts and ends with him. He wrote the book. He is everything to do and not to do in the business.' But at the age of nine all Bruce saw was the 'what to do' and he was totally inspired by the man, the music and the working-class-rebel-hero image.

Immediately after this Bruce persuaded his mother to get him a guitar (they ended up renting one), but at the age of nine he wasn't quite ready and talked about how his hand was 'too small to get into it. Besides, guitar lessons at the time were like a coma, buzzing on the B-string. I *knew* that wasn't the way Elvis did it.' Eventually Bruce did embark on the same course as Elvis, checking out all the music within earshot and paying attention to what he liked.

Initially, everything he heard was contemporary, via the radio or TV, but later he became more analytical and historically minded. However, he was fortunate because that rush, that *feeling* which he always refers to, was at its peak when Bruce first parked himself by the radio. Aside from Elvis, he might tune into Chuck Berry, Buddy Holly, as well as the melodramatic teen-idols that followed the demise of the early greats. He took it all in, but selectively, as evidenced by the cover tunes he performs in concert. As he got more involved in music, the times and the tunes became even more dynamic, and the pop music of the early Sixties became the foundation of his musical inspiration. The sounds of Phil Spector led to Gary U.S. Bonds, Mitch Ryder etc., until Dylan came along and opened some real lyrical and stylistic doors. The Beatles pushed them all the way open.

Like Elvis, the Beatles came to Bruce via Ed Sullivan, followed by a flood of radio hits. The significance of these facts weren't lost on Bruce who not only understands the power of the music itself but also the crucial importance of its distribution through the mass media. Rock was the music made for a teen audience and that — along with films and TV — was about the only cultural offering that meant anything to Bruce and most kids. In a situation where the study of art was relegated to fifteen minutes per day (and where Bruce once fulfilled an assignment to draw a picture of Christ by showing Him crucified on a guitar!), rock was the voice of a culture which Bruce felt he needed to be part of. He's talked about the situation on several occasions saying things like, 'I wasn't brought up in a house where there was a lot of reading and stuff. I was brought up on TV. Who was William Burroughs? They never brought him up in high school in the Sixties — unless you were hanging around with that kind of crowd. And I didn't hang around with no crowd that was talking about William Burroughs.' Hitting even harder on the medium and the message, Bruce said 'When I was growing up, the only thing that never let me down was rock 'n' roll. Like rock 'n' roll came to my house when there seemed no way out. It just seemed like a dead-end street. It reached down into all those homes where there was no music or books or any kind of creative sense, and it infiltrated the whole thing. That's what happened in my house.' Springsteen is also excruciatingly conscious of the liberating force of music; 'Rock 'n' roll, man, it changed my life. It was like, you know, the 'Voice of America', the *real* America, coming

into your home. It was liberating, the out, the key out of the pits. Once I found the guitar I had the key to the highway!'

He says that the first time he could stand what he saw in the mirror was the day he had a guitar in his hand. That fateful day took place when he was thirteen, when his fever for baseball was abating and his love of music was on the rise. After his first negative experience with the guitar he decided that this time he wanted to be a drummer. Unfortunately, he couldn't afford a kit, but could just scrape enough money together for a pawn shop guitar — and the rest, as they say, is history. 'When I got the guitar I wasn't getting out of myself. I was already out of myself and I did not dig me. I was getting into myself.' The guitar gave him an identity ('so the heavies couldn't look right through me'), a weapon ('I bombed 'em with the blues') and a voice ('I learned how to make it talk'), but more than all this it was 'the gigantic motivator'. If there's one thing that continues to separate Springsteen from his musical contemporaries it's his emphasis on the positive and triumphal spirit of rock music. He recognizes the difference between positive and optimistic, and feels the need to produce positive effects while dealing with what is sometimes objectively quite negative material. He states the case succinctly: 'Rock 'n' roll's never about giving up. For me — for a lot of kids — it was a totally positive force, not optimistic all the time, but positive. It was never — never about surrender.' To this day, Springsteen continues to reaffirm that idea in his music.

Bruce has made the 'no surrender' ethos part of his personal philosophy and, in the face of a lot of misunderstandings and outright antagonism, has remained true to himself and to the music. If he saw the basic message as 'let freedom ring' then he also realized early on that the price of freedom is not only constant vigilance but constant practise. He talks about being an isolated teenager and how there was 'a certain involuntariness' to it. Since, for various reasons, he wasn't socially in demand, he turned this into a positive factor in his musical development. Eventually he became good enough on the guitar to be sought after, but by then he says he was immune to the social pressures and attitudes of his peers, and had for the most part lost his desire to be part of any clique or group.

There was one exception. That was a band called The Castiles which Bruce was eager to join as soon as he became aware of their existence. By the time he reached eighth grade Bruce had had enough of Catholic school and convinced his parents to send him to Freehold Regional, a public school. It was around that time that Bruce picked up the guitar for real, and it was through a high school acquaintance named George Theiss, who was leader of the band, that Bruce finally got an invitation to play. The story goes that Theiss was actually more interested in Bruce's sister Ginny but after a lot of pressure from the other band members who were looking for a guitarist, he finally remembered to mention the group to Bruce one night. Up to that point Bruce had been playing solo with the radio and he literally jumped at the opportunity. The full account of Bruce's introduction to the band is recounted in *Born To Run*, with the tale told by The Castiles' factory worker

manager, 'Tex' Vineyard. In Tex's story the picture of Bruce's determination emerges, starting with this 'kid' (acne-faced and all) who shows up one night in the middle of a torrential downpour to audition, doesn't really know any *songs* (just snatches that he's picked up off the radio) and who was told to come back when he actually knew a few. Well...the next night Bruce came back and, as Tex put it, played five leads that would blow your ears. It was shocking enough progress in one day, but even more impressive because he had learned them all by himself from the radio. As Miami Steve would say later, 'Bruce has a real *fast* ear.' After this demonstration of guitar prowess, Bruce was welcomed into the band and The Castiles became the focus of his personal and social life during his high school years. Bruce later recalled that the best thing that ever happened to him was when he got thrown out of the first band he was in, and went home and put on *It's All Over Now* by the Rolling Stones and learned the guitar solo. It was probably his Castiles audition.

Throughout this period Bruce's awareness of the outside world was also increasing dramatically, and exploration and escape became his two main modes. As a little kid he wandered the streets and alleys, hung out on the boardwalks and beaches and saw a good part of Jersey on excursions with his Dad. This trend continued into adolescence when, aside from playing in the band, he would take off with a 'guy or two, maybe a girl' and seek escape from New Jersey and connection with the rest of the world, specifically the world of New York City. At first he didn't get much past the Port Authority where the bus dropped him off, but when he got older he and his friends would take off for weekends, spending nights on beaches and beach house roofs, and making more extensive inroads into New York City. By the time he was sixteen, he was also auditioning and playing solo all over New York and New Jersey, and these adventures formed the basis for most of the material on Bruce's first two albums. In particular, the song *Growin' Up* captures Bruce's rebellious and expansive spirit: 'I hid in the clouded wrath of the crowd but when they said, "Sit down", I stood up/Ooh...growin' up. Ooh...growin' up.' He didn't *want* to be an outsider, he just saw the limits and felt compelled to transcend them. And maybe be embraced for *that*.

21

# TWO

# DANCING
# IN THE DARK

Once Bruce was in a band, his concentration hardly wavered. He refused to lose faith and never let go of that startling vision of Elvis on the TV. The Castiles quite self-consciously followed The Beatles and took to wearing uniforms, playing Beatles covers, as well as songs by The Who, The Rolling Stones and the best of the British invaders. They also started writing their own songs and Bruce says he was lucky in that he learned fairly early 'that you have to write your own material'. In the beginning though, the main problem was choosing the tunes they covered, for it was unusual to even consider doing original songs in any of the New Jersey club or dance venues. Even in New York there were just a handful of clubs that featured artists performing their own songs, though Bruce discovered them early on and made a point of playing them when the time came.

Largely due to their song choices, The Castiles' set wasn't exactly par for a Friday night out in Freehold or Point Pleasant. However, it was also partly due to the polarized social scene — a schism that was also economic, geographical and somewhat superficial. The Castiles were playing both inland and on the Shore to both 'greasers' and 'frats' whose differences extended to the types of music they would tolerate. By treading a middle ground the band usually managed to offend both audiences, with the 'greasers' preferring the soul part of the set, and rejecting the British sounds which the 'frats' preferred. From that experience Bruce realized that you can't please all the people all of the time, but forced to confront this cultural and class-oriented polarity at such an early point, he also chose to take most of his characters and images from the inland, disenfranchised 'greaser' world. These are the working-class people who race and work on cars when they're not working in factories and where the conflicts are sharper and more inescapable, therefore more dramatic. (Bruce also chose his peers as his audience, and though he didn't totally fit the bill, if you'd met him as a teen you would have *seen* a 'greaser'.) He has attempted on several occasions to explain his songs and makes a point that is frequently overlooked; 'The *subject* I sing about is not

necessarily what I sing about. I'll use situations and probe for the very basic emotions. The conflicts I sing about are present in every level of life from the street level to the business level.'

Springsteen has become increasingly conscious of his own songwriting process and his aims, but being almost totally self-taught he also realized early on the combination of elements that make the best songs (and art). On the tendency of most fledgling songwriters to literally follow the dictim 'write about what you know' he warns: 'You do that and this is what happens. First you write about struggling along. Then you write about making it professionally. Then somebody's nice to you. You write about that. It's a beautiful day, you write about that. That's about twenty songs in all. Then you're out. You got nothing to write.'

Along with becoming a songwriter, he began to develop a reputation as a kick-ass guitar player, thereby shocking lots of Jerseyites when his first album came out on which he was not only a *singer* but also a lively performer. His experience with The Castiles was probably most valuable in terms of performance, since the band played consistently for several years and in a variety of situations including supermarket openings, CYO (Catholic Youth Organization) dances and beneath the screen of *The Russians Are Coming, The Russians Are Coming.* Bruce recalls: 'We used to play the Elks Club, the Rollerdome and the local insane asylum. One time this guy in a suit got up and introduced us for twenty minutes saying we were greater than The Beatles. Then the doctors came up and took him away.' He's also got some great Mafia stories from later days.

Bruce also decided early on that he wasn't in it for the money and made the rather pertinent comment that if he 'was writing songs to become a businessman, I'd become a businessman.' This is in keeping with observations made by others, specifically John Hammond Sr., that Bruce 'is the only person I've met who cares absolutely nothing about money'. What he does care about is keeping control over his music and his career and though initially he made a lot of mistakes, certain tendencies were obvious from his earliest 'professional' days. Even with Tex Vineyard as

The Castiles' manager, most of the initiative came from Bruce and George Theiss, including the idea to record a single, which they did in May, 1966. They paid a steep fifty dollars an hour for studio time in the Bricktown Mall and reportedly wrote the songs, *Baby I* and *That's What You Get*, on the way to the session. With the cost of the hour foremost in their minds, they didn't stop when Bruce's E-string broke and tore through the songs relatively undaunted. Later in his career Bruce went to the opposite extreme by using the cheapest studio time (which produced another set of problems), but he's kept the habit of arriving at the studio with the ink on his songs still wet, and has always favored a live recording approach.

That early single never materialised and it isn't clear that they had any plan to go any further with recording anyway.

Around that time through his forays into Manhattan, Bruce discovered a lively music scene in Greenwich Village. The year was 1967 and he took his intelligence back to Tex who was sceptical about the possibility of getting them any gigs, but decided to give it a try since they

clearly had their hearts set on it. It was the obvious next step for a band that had been playing Jersey for four years. What follows is Gordin 'Tex' Vineyard's account care of Dave Marsh.

'Shit, there were ten thousand bands in New Yawk but the boys said "Aw Tex, you gotta try for us." Finally I called the Cafe Wha? — that was on the same street with the Night Owl, where the Lovin' Spoonful were getting started, the Mothers of Invention and the Fugs. Anyway, I called for an audition. "Naw" they said, "we ain't auditioning nobody. We got a hunnert bands to audition, and we only got thirty nights open for the rest of the winter." But finally I convinced them to at least hear us.

'So we got there, and everybody's real nervous. But Bruce, he says to Curt, the bass player, "I want some good lead bass. Not plunk, plunk but lead — with a pick." He came out with *My Generation* and I hate to say this but we got twenty-nine out of thirty bookings.'

Well, they killed *My Generation* but the qualities that made The Castiles standouts across the river and down the

coast didn't exactly stand New York on its head, and they finished their Cafe Wha? gigs without any recognition. This 'bigtime' experience came at a crucial point for Bruce, since high school graduation soon followed. Tex recalls that most of the other Castiles were thinking about college or marriage but Bruce remained resolutely on course. A few years before, when all the other band members had taken jobs, Tex suggested that maybe Bruce ought to get one too. At that point Bruce dramatically jumped into Marion Vineyard's lap and told her that Tex had said a dirty word — work. Bruce sensed that any outside job (like marriage) was a trap and he avoided them with a vengeance. (The myth has it that he never worked at all, though he had a few 'small jobs'.) It was clear to everyone by then that music was Bruce's vocation and he had made his position clear to all the people closest to him. His

parents were never convinced he could make it, but people like Tex and Marion Vineyard supported him, both financially and by providing crucial moral support. Meanwhile, there were larger issues demanding Bruce's attention; one of which was the Vietnam War. Bruce was of draft age and decided to enroll in Orange County College primarily to avoid the draft. When he realized that he might be able to beat it without an educational deferment and could then concentrate on music, he lost little time in leaving school. By this time Bruce had been playing solo gigs in both New Jersey and New York and he met a 'New York record producer' who advised him that he could easily beat the draft, and besides, he was guaranteed a recording contract any day. The contract never materialized but Bruce did manage to stay out of the Army. He

went into the draft board, answered yes to all questions, 'even said I was a homo' and was told to go home.

Bruce was not immune to the social and political forces of the late Sixties, but he was living a fairly isolated life, increasingly focused on a group of musicians who'd gravitated to a club called The Upstage in Asbury Park. Here he found something of a spiritual home, a place to play, hang out and meet other musicians, and it amounted to a dream come true. All of his practising had paid off and when he made his entrance, he was soon recognized as the hottest guitarist on the scene. By the time he'd discovered the Upstage, he'd formed a band called Earth which was loosely based on Cream; a trio with a similar heavy blues sound. And though Bruce stuck with roughly the same sound for some time, when he started hanging out at the Upstage he had his pick of fellow players and Earth was soon dissolved in favor of other associations.

If the Upstage has been mythologized there is good reason; most of the musicians later known as E Streeters and Asbury Jukes either met there or through people that had met there. Aside from developing a particular sound, image and ethos, the cast of characters formed a kind of mutual support society which lasted through the immediate lean years and is still a formidable bond. What follows is Springsteen's description of the club, taken from the liner notes of Southside Johnny's first album:

There was a lotta musicians there, 'cause the bands that came down from North Jersey and New York to play in the Top Forty clubs along the shore would usually end up there after their regular gig, along with a lotta different guys from the local areas. Everybody went there 'cause it was open later than the regular clubs and because between one and five in the morning, you could play pretty much whatever you wanted, and if you were good enough, you could choose the guys you wanted to play with.

'The Upstage was run by this beat-type guy named Tom Potter who plastered the walls with black lights and pin-ups and showed Fifties smokers to the kids in between bands...It was a great place. He'd slip you five or ten bucks to sit in and you could work it out so you'd never have to go home, 'cause by the time you got out of there it was dawn and you could just flop on the beach all day, or you could run home before it got too light, nail the blankets over the windows of your room and just sleep straight through till the night.'

Bruce's description continues, and he names some names that appear on some albums including his own.

'There were these guys...Mad Dog Lopez, Fast Eddie Larachi, his brother Little John, Margaret and the Distractions (house band). Black Tiny, White Tiny, Miami Steve and assorted E Streeters plus the heaviest drummer of them all, in terms of both poundage and sheer sonic impact. Biiiiig Baaaaad Bobby Williams, badass king of hearts, so tough he'd go to the limit for you every time, all night. You will never see most of these names on another record besides this one, but nonetheless, they're names that should be spoken in reverence at least once, not 'cause they were great musicians (truth is, some of them couldn't play nothin' at all) but because they were each in their own way

a living spirit of what, to me, rock and roll is all about. It was music as survival and they lived it down in their souls, night after night. These guys were their own heroes and they never forgot.'

Springsteen never forgot either and those days are echoed in lyrics (*Prove It All Night*), in the names of musical characters, in the fact that he still haunts some of the same Jersey clubs, and most importantly, in his belief in the spirit and the meaning of the music and the act of playing it.

It seems that even back then Bruce's talents were obvious, and the band that followed Bruce's arrival at the Upstage was formed on the invitation of drummer Vini 'Mad Dog' Lopez ('just out of jail...says he's lookin' for a guitarist') and organ player Danny Federici ('wearing a three-quarter length black leather jacket, very greaser, and his wife Flo had on a blonde wig'). Federici in turn remembers Bruce in his classic leather jacket with his guinea T, but even more that he was '*so fast*', adding that he never plays like he used to play. (Springsteen would later explain that the 'concept of taste had not yet entered my thinking'.)

Bruce went along with them and, with the addition of bass player Vinny Roslyn, they called the group Child. Shortly thereafter they got wind of a Long Island band with the same name and changed theirs to Steel Mill. That idea came from a friend named Chuck Dillon, but the decision to go with it was Bruce's, who was accepted as The Boss way back then. (Gary Tallent mentioned a couple of key points when he talked about how 'a bunch of us used to get together at a club called the Upstage and jam for two hours on *I'm A Man*. We formed bands. We always thought Bruce was a good act. If there was any chance of making a living through music, we figured it would have to happen through him.')

Steel Mill went on to become the premier group of Bruce's pre-recording days. They were the longest lived, most widely exposed, most popular, and in an odd way, progressive. The band's sound is usually described as being pre-heavy metal, but if nothing else Bruce's guitar playing and lyric writing kept them away from the clichés of a genre that was still developing. His playing was still fast, but it could be melodic, and his style was typically hybrid with its rockabilly accents and Chuck Berry-style riffs. Steel Mill was immensely popular on the Jersey coast, with a beat and energy that were a lot more in tune with the local lifestyle than were the psychedelic sounds originating from the opposite coast. In fact, it was during Steel Mill's early days that Douglas Springsteen heard the call of the West and moved his family to San Mateo, California. Bruce refused to go along — for a variety of reasons — not least of which was that he'd carved a niche for himself in New Jersey's indigenous music scene and was reluctant to start over.

After his family's move, Bruce lived in their old house until he was finally evicted, and from that point on he lived in a variety of situations. He spent some time living above the surfboard factory of friend and Steel Mill manager Carl Virgil 'Tinker' West, a Californian, who finally taught

Bruce how to drive on a trip to his native state. Bruce was nineteen at the time the band made this momentous journey, and the irony of how old he was before he learned to drive hasn't been lost on many of his fans. It was also on this trip that Bruce earned the nickname 'The Gut Bomb King' thanks to his diet of junk food. All the stories about Bruce living on cheeseburgers, Pepsi and Drakes cakes were true, though now he maintains a healthy and fairly strenuous regimen which includes eating vegetables, long distance running and weightlifting. But, says Bruce, 'I'm no fanatic. I still like to eat in diners.'

Bruce also got a case of culture shock when they arrived to play a New Year's Eve gig at the Esalen Spa near Big Sur. Said Bruce: 'I've never been outta New Jersey in my life and suddenly I get to Esalen and see all these people walkin' around in sheets. I see someone playing bongos in the woods and it turns out to be this guy who grew up around the corner from me'. Apparently the bongo player got a better reception though, because Bruce summed up the experience by saying that 'Nobody wanted to listen to a guy with a guitar.'

Back in New Jersey, Steel Mill had left an ever growing group of fans and even some effusive reviews. They had performed up and down the eastern seaboard and had a particularly strong connection with Richmond, VA. This may have had something to do with singer Robin Thompson of Richmond's Mercy Flight, who was eventually drafted to replace Bruce on vocals; Bruce was still insecure about his voice and wanted to concentrate on his guitar playing. It was also at that point that a certain Miami Steve was brought in as bass player, and the band was a solid enough unit to contemplate an en masse move to Richmond. The move did not come about, but they did make another journey to California, this time playing in San Francisco which they found particularly receptive. San Francisco Examiner writer Philip Elwood did a major review of one of their shows, stating that he'd never been so overwhelmed by a totally unknown band and that 'they deserve and demand attention'. The article attracted the attention of entrepreneur Bill Graham, who invited the band to make an audition tape for a possible recording contract. Three songs were recorded: *He's Guilty* also known as *The Judge Song, Goin' Back To Georgia* and *Train Ride*, but Graham was only moderately interested and offered the band a meager $1,000 advance which they wisely refused. Needless to say, Graham later regretted his offer and, for a time, Steel Mill may have also regretted passing it up because the spark was largely gone by the time they returned to New Jersey.

The band played more gigs that summer to wildly enthusiastic local crowds but during the summer of 1970 race riots hit Asbury Park and the rest of New Jersey. As Miami Steve put it, the town went down the tubes and 'we went right down with it'. A final blow came when a packed gig at an outdoor swim club was stopped nearly as soon as it began by Police Chief McCarthy, whose good work on behalf of the band was rewarded by them adding a special 'Chief McCarthy' card to their infamous Monopoly game. (It allowed the bearer to throw anyone in jail for no reason

at all.) Due to these developments and Bruce's desire for a change in music and format, the group finally played its last show in January '71 at the Upstage Club.

Throughout this rather rough period the Upstage continued to be a focal point, and during the long, cold and poverty-stricken winter that Bruce spent miserably writing songs, he also began working on a plan that would define the form of his musical outings for several years. He conceived of a ten piece group, 'with horns and girl singers' that would allow him to explore the combinations of his favorite rock, soul and R&B sounds. He formed a group called Dr. Zoom and the Sonic Boom, which was a stop gap and a chance to have fun while they looked for the horn players and the girl singers. Dr. Zoom was one of the most egalitarian of all Bruce's efforts, formed with the intention of including all the people who 'weren't in a band' along with people who just couldn't play. Provision was made for non-players by placing a Monopoly board and chairs at center stage, and chaos was the order of the day. As Bruce described it: 'Somebody'd take a solo and we'd all fall down laughing'. And that was a main purpose behind Dr. Zoom; to restore the fun and craziness that has been eroded by the long and frustrating stint as Steel Mill.

In the meantime more serious efforts were made to form the ten piece group, and Bruce finally found a place in the band for bass player Gary Tallent — after Miami Steve was put back on guitar duties. Tallent had spent so much time just watching Bruce play, 'pulling a chair right up in front and just staring at me', that he was finally recognized. Miami recalls the educational process. 'We spent six months getting the guys. That was the first time that we ever found out that — forget rock 'n' roll — there's no such thing as rhythm and blues horn players. At least in our area, with the white guys; they all wanted to do jazz.' They did find one jazz piano player with classical training as well, who happened to be black and named David Sancious. Sancious was an integral part of the early E Street band — with his home address serving as the name — but he wouldn't last as long as the rock 'n' roll horn player that they finally found. Clarence Clemons is not only an incredible sax player and thus responsible fo the immediate recognizability of the band's early work, he's also Bruce's ultimate on-stage foil and pastmaster of pantomime. Bruce tells several stories (different versions) of their first meeting and always the point is somehow made that they were lucky as hell to end up with Clarence on their side and that once he was in, the force was with them and sparks began to fly. (The sense of luck isn't one-sided, since Clarence once described his early life as 'my search for Bruce'.)

The history of the first official Bruce Springsteen Band is also recounted from the stage in only slightly dramatized terms. Bruce talks about how they finally got the big band together, then they lost a couple of members, kicked out a few more and how when it comes to splitting hot-dogs five ways 'you get down to your boys'. The boys he got down to were the first ones he turned to when opportunity came but, by the end of 1971, the reality was that it was down to one boy. Springsteen was on his own, but the spark was there and he was lookin' to start a fire.

Clarence Clemons and eyepatch

# THREE
# PROVE IT ALL NIGHT

For all Bruce Springsteen's avowed faith in music, there have been hard times to try him. He's commented that music should always be fun, although it's never easy, but by the time 1972 rolled around, he wasn't even having much fun. Bruce had taken to playing solo again, which he did whenever the going got rough, he needed money or was without a band. This time he went all the way out to California looking for a change of scene, and even though he found this place in San Diego Bay 'where they play guitars all night and all day', most of the players he met were fourteen or fifteen-year-old kids playing in garages, which suddenly made what he'd left back in New Jersey look a lot more promising. Besides, when he told people he was from New Jersey and the reaction was 'yech', Bruce may have discovered a spark of pride and identity that he hadn't previously realized. Kind of like Dorothy, in the *Wizard Of Oz*, he spent all that time escaping only to 'find it all' in his own backyard. And after his return he was able to make some progress in the crucial business side of what was starting to look like a career.

These days, most everyone is aware of Bruce Springsteen's roots in New Jersey. They've been stressed in relation to his imagery, his identity, his musical influence etc., but what's hard to realize is that the backwaters inhabited by Bruce and his fellow E Streeters were psychologically a million miles away from the nearby metropolitan areas of New York and Philadelphia. It's true that as time went on the individual band members — most notably Steve Van Zandt — made inroads into the professional music scene, but they were still quite naive and out of touch with the machinations of The Industry. As Miami explained: 'We weren't big door knockers', and the people who knocked on *their* doors were mostly small time hustlers. Two of these were introduced to Bruce by Tinker West, the songwriting and production team of Mike Appel and Jim Cretecos. They had large ambitions but fairly small credentials; one production credit for Sir Lord Baltimore and the dubious honor of having penned a hit song for the Partridge Family. Apparently billing themselves as manager-producers, they convinced Bruce to sign a combination management and production contract to the tune of fifteen percent and five albums to be made for their own Laurel Canyon Music. The signing of the significant document was supposedly done on the hood of a car in the unlighted parking lot of a bar. While the location is a myth, the fact is that Bruce didn't care much about money but did care about getting his music out, so the deal begins to seem plausible — especially when he describes the economic and psychological dilemmas related to not being booked because they insisted on playing what they liked and 'because we never did any Top 40. *Never*. In the midst of this frustration, Bruce jumped at the first thing that looked like an opportunity. 'The kicks started to wear off and a lot of the time we didn't make enough to eat. That's why I signed with Mike (Appel). Anything was better than what was happening at the time.'

Mike Appel has been one of the most maligned figures in Bruce's life, and there are a few good reasons for this. A former Marine sargeant, Appel was notoriously brusque and abrasive, and when it was later discovered that he'd grossly mishandled Bruce's interests, he didn't find too many friends with Bruce s fans. But Appel also had two qualities that were essential for Bruce at the time; he had a total belief in Bruce's talent and, as Bruce described it, he was 'responsive', and the encouragement was badly needed at that time. And while Appel's extreme comments and actions frequently made him appear way off the mark (he considered himself a sort of John The Baptist to Bruce's Christ), with hindsight it appears that he *was* something of a prophet. Appel would later be compelled to remind employees at CBS that 'Bruce Springsteen isn't a rock act. He's a religion.' From the very beginning Appel was in touch with the fundamentals of that faith, saying 'Look, there was never any doubt in my mind that he was one of the greatest. Onstage in that leather jacket...like Elvis. We all want a piece of that leather.' So Appel and Cretecos got a piece and began to develop and hustle it. They loved Bruce's songs — for which they were also to be the publishers — and if he wasn't already prolific enough they'd invite him to their office in New York knowing that since he traveled by bus he was sure to write at least one new song before he hit the Lincoln Tunnel. Soon Appel was comparing Bruce to everybody from Shakespeare and Keats (though Yeats might have been more on target) to Bob Dylan, and even went so far as to bill himself as the next Albert Grossman (Dylan's original manager).

The next thing to do was to get Bruce that mythical recording contract, and it's here that several versions of a crucial story emerge. It's been acknowledged by all concerned that Appel discussed everything with Bruce, so there are some questions about just what their actual strategy was, and who was the prime strategist. The first decision was to target CBS Records, which had not only been Dylan's label but also had a good reputation for selling records. Some say that Appel went directly to CBS President Clive Davis, but being unable to reach him, 'settled' for John Hammond Sr., the most famous talent scout in music history who'd 'coincidentally' signed Dylan.

The story goes that Bruce just happened to be reading Anthony Scaduto's biography of Dylan, so at least he knew who Hammond was. What seems more likely considering Appel's (and Springsteen's) fascination with Dylan, was that they intentionally sought out Hammond. But at that point it was Appel's ballgame and his gung-ho qualities that did the trick. Hammond's secretary recalls urging him to make an appointment with Appel and Springsteen because Appel 'came on very strong', and Hammond decided it was worth fifteen minutes of his time. Many years later in a classic interview by a nine-year-old, Bruce responded to the question, 'How did you get to be a rock and roll star?' with two answers.

'Oh, let me see, it wasn't easy. Well there are two stories to that. One is that I ran into this guy that knew this guy that got me into this big building, this record company, and I went up and auditioned by myself with a guitar...that's one story.'

The second one he tells is a variation on the mythical meeting with a space man or a gypsy in which a wish is granted, but what actually went down when he 'auditioned by myself with a guitar' has become equally mythologized.

When Mike and Bruce got to Hammond's office, Appel reportedly opened with, 'You're the guy who discovered Bob Dylan huh? Well, we want to find out if it was just luck or if you really have ears'. To this the genteel Hammond replied, 'Stop, you're making me hate you.' Springsteen was initially pretty calm, figuring that 'nothin'' would happen', but 'I went into a state of shock as soon as I walked in. Before I ever played a note Mike starts screamin' and yellin' 'bout me. I'm shrivelin' up and thinkin'. "Please Mike, give me a break. Let me play a damn song". So dig this, before I ever played a note the hype began.' Finally Hammond cut Appel off, asked Bruce to play and he responded with either *It's Hard To Be A Saint In The City* or *Growin' Up* depending on who's telling the story. Hammond's response to this kid on guitar was undeniable, and even more impressive considering that he'd 'discovered' such artists as Bessie Smith, Billie Holiday and Bob Dylan. Said Hammond: 'I couldn't believe it. I reacted with a force I've felt maybe three times in my life. I knew at once that he would last a generation.' Hammond began to act immediately, scheduling Bruce into a club called the Gaslight for that evening as a kind of second audition for some of the other CBS brass. This got a response that was a harbinger of worse things to come, the likes of, 'Well, he looks so much like Dylan that he must be a copy of him'. Hammond refuted this connection at every turn, though the association was to plague Bruce for years — largely thanks to his recording company's lack of vision. The other thing that Hammond did was to have a lawyer look over Bruce's contract with Appel which he pronounced 'a slavery deal'. But Bruce was bound to both Appel and their agreement and, while Hammond arranged both a relatively generous recording budget and advance, the contract worked out between Appel and CBS on Bruce's behalf only bound him further to his 'slavery' deal. While he was committed to Appel for five albums, he was signed to CBS for ten, and he received only a fraction of the royalty rate that Appel and Co. were to be paid by CBS. But the man who cared nothing about money did care about getting his band back together and going into the studio to record an album. That, after all, was the whole point.

In his discussions with Bruce, Hammond had asked him about his musical history and if he'd ever played solo, to which Bruce replied that he'd been in rock groups for eight years, and had been playing for two months on his own. Perhaps because of the intensity and intimacy of hearing Bruce perform his songs alone on acoustic guitar, Hammond (and to a slightly lesser degree, Appel) were surprised and disgruntled when Bruce showed up with a full-tilt rock 'n' soul band behind him. As Springsteen put it: 'They forgot about the eight years and went with the two months'.

This misreading of what Bruce was about caused more than a few problems around the recording and promotion of his first album, though the discrepancy between 'rock Bruce' and 'folk Bruce' did incline John Hammond to make the prophetic comment that he looked forward to the day when Bruce would make a 'pure' album in the folk style, which just about describes *Nebraska*.

Part of the confusion was the result of Bruce introducing his songs in person, performing solo on acoustic guitar (or sometimes on piano as on his CBS demo tape), which tended to draw attention to the moodiness of his pieces. Such an impression was generally positive, but it excluded Bruce's awareness of each song's possibilities and also obscured the point that he was essentially a rocker, no matter what the surface style, tempo or instrumentation. Since Appel and Cretecos were producing the album, the difference in their approach to the material was quite significant. Bruce finally brought Appel most of the way around to seeing and hearing his vision, but Appel admits that initially 'perhaps I was too caught up in his lyrics. When Bruce came in and played me *Spirit In The Night* on guitar, I liked the song, but I didn't extend the tune into the band backing. Bruce said, "It's just because you listened to it on the guitar. You can't tell exactly how it will sound."'

The other major reason for the confusion was that a

It's hard to be a saint in the city – but Bruce does his best

number of so-called 'singer-songwriters' had emerged in the early Seventies, most of whom played mellow music with innocuous and personal lyrics. Being perceived as a member of that group did initially help Bruce to get a foot in the door, but it had its repercussions. As soon as he opened his mouth and the band started to play, the similarities instantly evaporated. Bruce had played both ends against the middle with the solo singer-songwriter image (since he'd observed that 'that's all people were buying at the time') but soon there were some prices to pay.

For a while Bruce's main concern was with 'Bruce Springsteen, band leader and proud owner of a recording contract'. He quickly reassembled the band, which at that point was scattered all over the eastern seaboard. Danny Federici and Steve Van Zandt couldn't make the recording due to prior commitments, but Van Zandt did manage to show up for one recording session, punching an amplifier to produce a perfect blast of feedback during *Lost In The Flood*. The rest of the band were able to drop what they were doing and join The Boss. *Greetings From Asbury Park, N.J.* as the album would be called, features 'Mad Dog' Lopez credited as Vincent 'Loper' Lopez, as well as Garry Tallent, Clarence Clemons (with his name mis-

Steve Van Zandt

34

spelled) and David Sancious on piano and organ. Bruce rejected the idea of hiring session players (alias 'hired-guns') but did employ Richard Davis on stand-up bass and Harold Wheeler on piano when he was sent back to the studio to come up with a possible single after the rest of the band had returned to their previous engagements.

The recording of *Greetings* took place under less than ideal circumstances. They recorded at a tiny studio called 914 in Blauvelt, N.Y., and though engineer Louis Lahav was up to spec, the facilities were not. It was also geographically inconvenient, but the price was right and since Appel was being paid as producer, any money saved on the $40,000 recording budget went back into Laurel Canyon and related enterprises. This turned out to be a case of rather warped and short-sighted priorities. Not that the album is unlistenable, but it was completed in only three weeks at a point when Springsteen could have used the time to perfect the arrangements and to learn more about the options offered by multi-track recording technology. To this day he still prefers recording as live as possible, although he inadvertently got a taste of what studio work could be about when the completed album was rejected by CBS for lack of a suitable single. More flexible in these matters than he would be later in his career, he returned to 914 to work on *Blinded* and *Spirit*, which very nearly turned out to be solo productions.

So Springsteen managed to record an album, and though it may not have been exactly what he wanted (he referred to it at one point as sounding like an aberration from a street poet), he did get a fairly lively sound which wasn't standard rock. He called the album *Greetings From Asbury Park, N.J.*, and used an expensive graphic of an oversized postcard of the resort town as part of his introduction to the world. It looked like a fairly good beginning for our hero, since with the backing of Clive Davis, Springsteen was one of CBS's top priorities. What that meant in terms of promotion should have helped guarantee Bruce instant and positive recognition, but there were some factors outside of his control that undermined his best efforts.

Rock music, which had only recently been such a unifying banner, was fragmenting in the early Seventies; the music being foisted on the public was of the alienated and self-oriented variety, with the distraction of Bowie and the dull thud of the heavy metalers defining the poles. So along comes Bruce Springsteen with a well grounded and positive perspective on life and he gets tagged as the 'New Bob Dylan' which commercially was like the kiss of death. All of which might not have been so bad if the obvious single from the album, *Spirit In The Night* hadn't been just a little too long to fit the confines of 'hit radio'. Thus the album got almost no airplay and was only recognized by those critics clear-minded enough to see beyond CBS' hype.

*Greetings* opens with *Blinded By The Light* which is actually more evocative of Dylan than anything else on the album, mainly due to the break-neck lyric delivery, quirky imagery, and unheard of rhyme scheme. Starting with the now famous 'madman drummers bummers and Indians in

the summer with a teenage diplomat', it begins to seem that if Springsteen hadn't used 'diplomat' (which hadn't been in the rock lexicon until *Like A Rolling Stone*), maybe the comparisons wouldn't have been so prevalent. When word of this started getting back to Bruce he reacted with praise for Dylan ('It's *the* greatest music ever written, to me. The man says it all, exactly the right way. Incredibly powerful. You don't get no more intense..'), but he also made the point that 'I go onstage and feel myself. And I'm not worried about, "oh man that note sounds like this dude. Hey man, I heard that word off *Subterranean Homesick Blues*." At one time it worried me but it doesn't anymore, because when I get onstage finally I feel myself. That's who I am.'

And it's who Springsteen is that really comes across on every song on *Greetings*. *Blinded By The Light* isn't likely to be compared to *Thunder Road* but it's got a great and humorous slant on the music business from a relatively new but inciteful arrival. With the commentary in this song ranging from 'hit them in the funny bone — that's where they expect it least' to the advice of 'save the buckshot turn up the band', it's clear that Springsteen's point of view was already quite developed by the time he made his first LP. This song, like *Growin' Up* which follows it, shows his penchant for pushing the limit, and thus he ends with the oft-quoted 'Mama always told me not to look into the sights of the sun/Oh but Mama that's where the fun is'.

*Growin' Up* is alternately funny and heavy as lead (from the guy with a 'boulder on my shoulder, feelin' kinda older') as well as containing some personal truth. Starting with the pose — 'I stood stone-like at midnight suspended in my masquerade/I combed my hair till it was just right and commanded the night brigade ' — the song moves through a fantastic series of actions to the final reconcilation of the lofty and earthly pulls on the singer who says, 'Well, my feet finally took root in the earth but I got me a nice little home in the stars.' He adds almost incidentally that 'I swear I found the key to the universe in the engine of an old parked car', and here it becomes clear that many of the themes, images, vocabulary and characters that would populate Springsteen's future work were already with him. The song, like *Blinded*, also shows Bruce as the rare emotive singer he is, using a half-spoken, half-sung style which can endow words with a multitude of meanings. It is the oldest song that Bruce still performs live and the spirit and the situations of the song still ring true and fresh.

The next song on the album, *Mary Queen Of Arkansas*, is the one album cut that made Bruce sound like a folk artist, mainly by virtue of its sparse guitar, the harmonica arrangement and his tortured singing. Unfortunately, it's lyrically and structurally quite weak, but it does give a glimpse of what Bruce must have sounded like to Hammond and Appel, and is the first example of the minimalist intensity that Bruce would exploit on the much stronger material of the *Nebraska* album.

*Does This Bus Stop At 82nd St.?* puts things back on track and is another lyrical bombardment, illuminating the 'urban' Bruce that so many critics would refer to. Luckily the album includes the lyrics so you can read them for

yourself, but with this song and the entire album, Bruce is like the people in the song who 'take out a full page ad in the trades to announce their arrival'. Bruce announces himself with the line spoken by Mary Lou when she's asked for the dope by the Daily News; 'Man the dope's that there's still hope'. That message is what really distinguished Bruce and his contribution. In the last line he refers to 'Señorita Spanish rose', who is named Maria and Rosalita later on, and thus a continuity is established in themes and characters, which is reinforced by David Sancious' elegant piano, creating a link between songs that makes the album work like a suite.

*Lost In The Flood* is structured like a suite (a form quite popular in the early Seventies) and is also extremely dramatic, hinting at the future songwriting qualities Bruce would develop. The song also reflects the malaise of the time with lines like 'Hey man, did you see that? His body hit the street with such a beautiful thud', at which point Bruce's voice comes through with the question, 'I wonder what the dude was sayin' or was he just lost in the flood?'. Bruce is trying to get through to his characters and his audience, starting with a soldier ('Hey gunner man, that's quicksand, that's quicksand that ain't mud/Have you thrown your senses to the war or did you lose them in the flood?') and moving on to a would-be typical character — 'That pure American brother, dull-eyed and empty faced/races Sundays in Jersey in a Chevy Stock super eight'. This brother's fate is oblivion and after describing a death where nothing is left of him, 'that is, nothin' left that you could sell', you get an indication of the cutting clarity that makes the narrator one of the survivors in a drowning world. Thematically this song is linked to much later work.

In *The Angel* Bruce took images from motorcycle and hot rod exploitation films, along with all those rock death songs, and almost succeeds in making them his own, with unprecedented lines like his description of the girlfriend as 'Madison Avenue's claim to fame in a trainer bra with eyes like rain'. *For You* follows as an even more convoluted and bizarre love story sung in the back of an ambulance, and while it's worth following the back and forth tale of this extreme relationship, it's the chorus that really stands out. It's also typical of Bruce's brand of respect, mixed with frustration. There's a large 'but' in the middle of the line 'I came for you, for you, I came for you, but you did not need my urgency'. This album also reflects Bruce's sense of urgency but some of the songs suffer from either lack of development or focus, though he can be excused for wanting to say everything. His own flood gates were bursting all over this first album.

Following a song whose subject's life is described as one long emergency, there is the relative sanity and adolescent purity of *Spirit In The Night*, which received the most attention and airplay and is the LP's most energetic and exuberant tune. It's also the one that earned Bruce the description of sounding like Bob Dylan with Van Morrison's back-up band, because it's got that soulful jazzy sound, and even a thematic affinity with some of Morrison's work, particularly *Moondance*. This one also has a full cast of characters whose names have usually been likened to

Chuck Berry's crew — no accident, since Bruce considers Berry one of rock's greatest lyricists. The song describes a magic evening with a bunch of friends piling into a car on a summer's night and heading off to Greasy Lake. What makes the song and what it describes so special is the spirit in the night; a combination of freedom, unity and release, and though the night has to end and too soon it's time to go, the repeated chorus suggests that the night should last forever. This is also one of Springsteen's first 'night' songs, and he's since reiterated in both song and conversation that it's 'his time of day'. Here he also claimed it as his artistic territory. Likewise, note the production which he gets almost total credit for.

From Greasy Lake ('about a mile down on the dark side or route eighty-eight') it's back to the city, takin' it all in, hustlin' and coming out with the cool observation that *It's Hard To Be A Saint In The City*. This tune is another travelogue narrated by the man/boy with 'skin like leather and the diamond hard look of a cobra', who could 'walk like Brando right into the sun'. He also claims to be so in tune that when he walks down the street he can hear its heart beat, and this is Bruce at his coolest and the music at its baddest. But even through a trip on the subways and past the cripple crying 'Nickels for your pity', it's clear that the saint has a heart as oversized as the postcard on the album jacket, and it's that quality in general that shines through and made the album a standout. Forget for a moment that *Greetings* was mishandled, had songwriting, arrangement and production problems, didn't get much in the way of airplay and only a fraction of the recognition it deserved. The main point was that Bruce announced himself loud and clear, and even if things didn't happen instantly he had a faith in himself and in the future. *Greetings* was recorded in 1972 and released in early '73 with the follow-up recorded and released by November of the same year. Compared to the pattern that fans have come to expect, this speed was phenomenal. In some ways it hurt him, which accounts in part for the later turnaround, but in the meantime there was a backlog of stuff to get out and a band to form and fine tune.

Bruce still didn't have things exactly his way, but he was working to get to that point and never lost sight of what it was about. He talks about how 'Even my mother when I told her I had a recording contract, said "What'll you call yourself now?" But who you are, it's obvious isn't it? The one thing I learned is to be real.' This sense of himself and what he was doing sustained him through steady and largely unhailed gigging, when these 'recording artists' were sleeping on attic floors during tours and were barely getting by financially. But through all the trials and tribulations they remained positive and self-confident. It may have been somewhat anti-climatic for a while, but as Bruce said, 'It was never a down. Me and Steve would always sit back and say, "As bad as this is right now, it will never be as bad as it was before we made an album or got a break." Who are we to complain, this is easy street. I'm lucky number one. It's a lot of work but you're always doing something you like. We always considered ourselves to be way in front of the whole ballgame.'

# FOUR

# LOST IN THE FLOOD

**The E Street Shuffle opens Bruce Springsteen's second album and conveys the anarchy, exuberance and comprehensive qualities of a band that was just finding itself, led by a man who was finally coming into his own. The song, like the album, treads a thin line between control and chaos, the same line that Bruce was walking at that very point, when he didn't have much professional leverage.**

Between the release of *Greetings* and *The Wild, The Innocent And The E Street Shuffle* Springsteen was hit left and right by events over which he had little influence. In May 1973 Clive Davis had been dethroned as President of CBS Records, and for political reasons it was not in Bruce's best interests to be perceived as a Davis ally. Bruce still had John Hammond on his side, but after the big Davis mandated push behind *Greetings* and its subsequent poor sales, Bruce's standing within the record company took a nose-dive. Some CBS personnel, who were not about to admit that the corporate publicity may have contributed to the negative reception, apparently relished the situation, and Mike Appel's increasingly tactless behavior managed to alienate Bruce even further from his record company. Since Appel and Cretecos had invested their life savings in Bruce's career they were greatly frustrated by the reception they now received at CBS. One story concerning Appel may hint at how extreme his reaction could become when his back was against the wall. Before *Greetings* was even released, Appel reportedly called the producer of that year's Super Bowl Festivities suggesting that instead of beginning the game with the usual *Star Spangled Banner*, they open the game with Bruce singing an original anti-war song called *Balboa Vs. The Beast Slayer*. Others say that Appel just wanted Springsteen to perform *The Banner*, but in either case Appel met the producer's refusal with a threat to put him out of a job. As usual, Appel's intentions were good but his method was distinctly counter-productive.

Throughout all this there were a few CBS employees who'd become devoted to Bruce, but even his most loyal fans had moments of discouragement that year. One of the low points came at the annual CBS convention in the summer, when like many a new act, Bruce was invited to play for the salesmen and their wives. Considering that this wasn't exactly the audience he was used to, and taking into account the recent negative reception he'd received at CBS, he was described as coming onstage with 'a chip on his shoulder'. According to John Hammond he played that way too, and he claims that 'People came up to me and said, "He really can't be that bad, can he, John?"'. Bruce's spirits may have been dampened slightly, but he retained some objectivity, realizing that these people were not the audience he sought. As he later described the scene, 'I followed Edgar Winter with his smoke bombs, and the salesmen loved that. So Danny and I did *Sandy* which I'd just written, just accordion and acoustic guitar. Then the band came out to play *Saint In The City*, *Thundercrack* and maybe another one. All these ladies in gowns in the front rows had their fingers in their ears, but I thought we played good, and so did Mike Pillote, Ron Oberman and Chip Monck. At least that's what they told me. What can I say?'

It was during 1973 that the band began the road work which was to form the real foundation of their popular success, and which sustained them through the hard times. Bruce was signed to Philip Morris for live bookings, and it was there that he found another ally and die-hard fan in the form of Barry Bell. (Bell still does Springsteen's bookings, though now they're both affiliated with Premier Talent.) Bell spoke to Dave Marsh about the early difficulties of booking Bruce, who could only be scheduled where he could sell tickets, which meant just a few towns on the East Coast. They did send him on a club tour of places that soon became home turf, most notably the Main Point in Philadelphia and Paul's Mall in Boston, along with the Quiet Knight in Chicago and Max's Kansas City in New York. In between, he'd play a few college dates, but because his reputation hadn't spread very far west, it was some time before he even reached the sympathetic audiences in Phoenix, Houston, Austin and Los Angeles. The critics were starting to come around; eventually they would be instrumental in getting people to Bruce's shows, and though no real groundswell had yet occurred, Bell recalls that 'All you had to do was read the newspaper and you would think that *Greetings* was the Number One album instead of number one thousand. Every time we booked him anywhere we got nothing but rave reviews.'

Bruce's stage shows not only changed with each tour, but nightly, and by that point he was already a showman. Faris Bouhafa, manager of Max's Kansas City during Bruce's stints there, mentioned the essential qualities of Bruce's stagecraft. 'The first shows (at Max's) were very spontaneous. Bruce has always done the street raps on stage and he always had an incredible sense of drama. After a while, every moment looked spontaneous, but he'd been doing it so long it had to be calculated.' Bruce may have been a seasoned performer, but he couldn't avoid all the pitfalls of being the new artist on the roster, even if he was an early favorite. In a well-intentioned(?) move to advance Bruce's career, Columbia sent him off as the opening act for a mini-tour by Chicago. They figured it would give him some exposure since Chicago was playing to sold-out arena crowds, but due to the fact that the two groups had totally different audiences, the opening act was subject to a more negative reaction than anything it'd experienced in a while. As Bruce described it, 'It was walk on the stage, blink, and that's it. It's hard to show an audience what a band's about in that little time. I couldn't stand it — everybody was so far away and the band couldn't hear me. Maybe if they had come to see me it would have been different. But I doubt it.'

Prompted by the frustration of playing to large halls as much as anything else, Bruce decided after that tour that he was gonna play by *his* rules. That meant no more opening act slots unless he could do his entire *two* hour show — a condition which made it a practical impossibility — and he firmly refused to play any more arenas or stadiums. These conditions further alienated Bruce from the corporate brass, though his uncompromising stance proved correct in the long run.

With all this temporarily behind him, Bruce and the band (Lopez, Federici, Clemons, Sancious and Tallent) headed back to Blauvelt and 914 Studios to make their second album. Speaking after the fact about what he was trying to do with *The Wild, The Innocent And The E Street Shuffle*, Bruce said that 'The new album was a little more what I wanted to do. There was more of the band in there and the songs were written more in the way I wanted to write.' Likewise, emphasizing his relationship to the group, henceforth known as The E Street Band, Bruce called the record a 'lazy hanging out summer album', recorded in 'the summer the band's consciousness started to develop. We were just waiting there, flashing on everything that was happening. I was exactly where I wanted to be. I had a band. I knew who I was. We were getting work. The album reflects that.'

*E Street* definitely has summer written all over it and as soon as you take a look at the sleeve notes it's obvious how much more the role of the band is stressed. Every player is credited on at least two instruments, along with everyone getting a 'background vocal' acknowledgement. On the LP Danny Federici plays accordian, which was actually his first instrument, and bassist Gary Tallent occasionally picks up a tuba at The Boss' urging. Here he makes a major contribution to the carnival sound that dominates a couple of songs from the first side. Bruce also lets on that he's a multi-instrumentalist since he plays 'all guitars, harmonica, mandolin, recorder' and of course, 'lead vocals'. There are also two cameo appearances, with Richard Blackwell playing congas and percussion (giving the first public hint of Mad Dog's inadequacy) and Albany 'Al' Tellone ('from Newark, N.J.') on baritone sax. It's all there on the jacket, along with mention of string arrangements, cornet, clavinet and second pianos — the trick is to sort it out as you listen.

Bruce was talking about starting to write like he wanted to, and also how 'On the second album I started to slowly find out who I am and where I wanted to be. It was like coming out of the shadow of various influences and trying to be yourself.' The band sound was definitely coming together, and aside from some instantly recognizable soul touches — the horns in particular — the band proved itself capable of following Bruce while forging its own identity. The other thing upon which the whole enterprise rested was Bruce's songwriting, which on the *E Street* album took some of the themes, subjects and characters of *Greetings* and stretched, bent, and in some cases took them all the way out. The album also clarified certain concerns which were only hinted at on *Greetings*. Escape and exploration run through the entire album, and the imaginative qualities of Springsteen's writing are taken to an extreme on *E Street*.

Its cinematic qualities are also more apparent than on *Greetings*, along with the epic sweep and grandeur which would dominate his style for the next LP as well. If the influence of the lavish production numbers of *West Side Story* are evident on this album, Bruce would choose grittier films like *Mean Streets* or *Badlands* as models for later LPs. Nevertheless, his sense of drama shines through, and with the band behind him, he was able to present two sides filled with a unique vision.

As an album, *The Wild, The Innocent And The E Street Shuffle* doesn't manifest the same level of artistic unity that would characterize his later work, but the way it begins does give some idea of how Bruce stood in relation to a 'hit' and 'hook' obsessed record industry. He blew a blue note right in their faces with the wake-up and tune-up intro to *The E Street Shuffle*. Almost as soon as his guitar comes in there's a sense that the song will come together, and it does — sort of. It was undoubtedly supposed to be loose, capturing the wild (and innocent) spirit of the man-child/boy-prophet and the rest of the kids who were making the E Street scene. In the process he hints at what in a live context becomes the band's tour de force, i.e. their ability to change tempo, style and intensity with a nod from The Boss and to do it all night and never the same way twice. This song became a prime example of how in performance the same words and melody may be transposed into any imaginable style, and *The E Street Shuffle* which is a meld of styles from blues to jazz, has been through most of them. Bruce's breathy delivery and strained intensity characterize the singing style he adopted for this LP, and *E*

*Street* is probably the most extreme example of it — he's literally out of breath.

One 'summer by the beach' tale runs into another, with images and a narrative again loosely derived from the world of Asbury Park — though Bruce says that most of the heavy personal stuff in his songs comes from spending time 'further up the beach'. This song includes the location in its title, though *4th Of July Asbury Park (Sandy)* is usually just called *Sandy*. In some ways it's a bridge between the more literal tales of the earlier albums and the more imaginative handling of material that would follow. The song is lengthy, a near epic by rock standards and much more narrative than most writers would attempt. It is also quite filmic, conveying the whole scope of 'little Eden', complete with costume descriptions and lighting cues. You can see the stone-like faces lit by the fireworks, and begin to understand the motivation for escape that this piece lays out more clearly than any previous song except *Growin' Up*. As with his 'first mate' in that song, what the singer wants is friendship as much as love (he comes to Sandy

after a waitress 'lost her desire for me') and the true innocence of it all — along with proof of Bruce's vocal mastery — is brought home with his rendering of the line 'Love me tonight, and I promise I'll love you forever'. The word 'forever' comes out like a swallowed question and it's the emotional heart of the song. It also recalls Bruce's description of high school dances where you weren't 'just asking a girl "Do you want to dance?" You were asking her, "Do you WANTA?" My life is in your hands.' That's why he'd get halfway across the dance floor and turn around, and it's why 'forever' gets all twisted. The song contains seeds of much that would follow; not just escape from the emptiness of the posers and the death in those (tomb)stone faces, but even the thematic analysis of America which compels him to set the song on the 4th of July — also known as *Independence Day*. It also shows Bruce as a more somber poet than *Greetings* indicated and prefaces the even more desperate continuation of this story in *Backstreets*. (The reference to Madame Marie, an actual fortune teller on the Asbury Boardwalk is also one of the

*Rosalita* comes to its climax

strongest indications of his tendency to employ both actual and fictional elements in his songs. His plug has also given Marie notoriety and loads of business over the years.)

In mood and character, *Kitty's Back* couldn't be much further away, but with the album title supplying one key to the unity of the material, here we have a reaction to a different kind of girl, and Kitty sounds like a wild one. She apparently had to come back, which may be bad for her, but it's good news for all the boys in this small unnamed town. On this LP, Bruce decided either to force the audience to listen harder to the words or someone convinced him to save some money by omitting the lyric sheet. While it is often sorely missed, you'd hardly have to understand anything but the chorus to get the idea of this one, where the music evokes the excitement that the song is about. Starting with a blues lick borrowed from Duane Allman or some such, it turns into a full-fledged rocker with soul instrumentation and breaks. Clarence shines on *Kitty*, as on the whole of side two, and all the boys are there at the mike for the 'oohs', which were fast becoming a trademark. (To be eclipsed in time by the 'one-two-three-four's.)

Kitty's return is followed by *Wild Billy's Circus Story* which is one of the most out-there tunes Bruce ever penned, both in terms of subject matter and arrangement. It's a rather long-winded tale of a down and out circus/carnival troupe with some descriptions (particularly of the Fat Lady) which are so funny they verge on parody. It might serve as a break before side two were it not overly long, though it's worth listening for the last line where the ring leader bids, 'all on board, next stop Nebraska'.

It's on side two that Springsteen's unity of vision becomes totally apparent for the first time. *Incident On 57th Street* sounds like it could be a Spanish Asbury after the race riots, or maybe Spanish Harlem, but more likely in Bruce's mind anyway, it is set on the West Side celebrated in *West Side Story*. The side works as a whole and, while there's a major contrast between the tone and the tales of *Incident* and *Rosalita*, there are also major changes in mood and point of view within the individual songs. (Bruce is unique in that his ballads are structurally more like short stories than songs, and at this point they were dense with images, characters and action.) *Incident* was also hailed as an example of Bruce's romanticism and poetry, and in that context it consolidates his theme of winners and losers while typically leaving the story open-ended. The tale of Spanish Johnny ('like a cool Romeo') and Puerto Rican Jane (who 'like a late Juliet...knew he'd never be true') moves through a late night meeting and salvation to a departure with a promise of return — 'maybe'. That 'maybe' draws you into the song even if you weren't already hooked on lines like Bruce as Johnny singing 'Hey little heroes summer's long but it ain't that sweet around here no more'. It's a matter of your own faith whether they'll 'find it out on the street tonight' or not. As proof that Bruce doesn't take himself (or his characters) too seriously, he'd done a rap break while performing *Incident* where he describes Johnny's departure in terms like 'he pulled on his pants. He pulled on his shirt. He pulled on his *tube* socks. The erstwhile hero even has trouble getting his car started, but finally the scales are tipped in favor of them getting away for 'one minute, one second'.

This beautiful ballad is paired with *Rosalita (Come Out Tonight)*, another set piece and rollercoaster narrative which continues with a Spanish character. This time it's Rosie, and she's trapped inside her house while Bruce comes serenading with a mission. He's come to confiscate her, liberate her, 'cause he wants to be her man. The way the singer talks her through what must be her own liberation is classic, telling her how closets are for hangers, windows are for cheaters and so on 'til he makes the point that she oughta walk out that door and to him. Aside from the driving music propelled by Clarence's sax, one of the patented Springsteen elements is that the promise of the singer is both generally and specifically tied up with music. That's what he has to offer and it's a true to life solution in Bruce's case — it's the only solution he personally knows. He presents it to her directly; 'But now you're sad, your mama's mad/And your papa says he knows that I don't have any money/Well, tell him this is his last chance/To get his daughter in a fine romance/Because the record company, Rosie/Just gave me a big advance'. This song is about those decisive moments, and as usual, Bruce is trying to convince one of his characters to take the leap, this time into his arms. Considering that the music is irresistible, she'd be a fool not to go along. Bruce often saves this tune for last and, if it seems effective on record, the live performance tears it to shreds. It's no accident that

*Rosalita* became the first concert video that CBS decided to release; it's guaranteed to whet anyone's appetite for the real thing.

Another tune that was frequently performed, is *New York City Serenade*, and while it's rich and sweet, the album version is somewhat muddled and continues for nine minutes, thus becoming something of an anti-climax. The most distinguished features are David Sancious' classical and jazz derived piano introduction and while there are some fine lines, only the choral 'Oh no, she won't take that train' and the final admonition to 'Listen to your junkman', stand out. Shades of the Beatles' *Goodnight* color the last few bars, which feature a rare example of a string arrangement on a Springsteen record.

Bruce was realizing where he was coming from, and others were beginning to understand as well, but *The Wild, The Innocent And The E Street Shuffle* is a difficult album to get a clear grasp of. The strengths of *Sandy, Incident* and *Rosalita* were clear to all who heard them but the rest of the album was uneven. All of these problems were cleared up and finally put to rest with the release of *Born To Run*, but there was a rather difficult period for Bruce to struggle through in the meantime. He would later say that he was born, grew old and died in the process, but since music had saved him, this was just his way of paying back the debt.

# FIVE

# HUNGRY HEART

If *Greetings* had been less than a commercial success, then *The Wild And The Innocent* was pretty much a disaster. Some critics had begun to come around but the LP received almost no airplay. As a result sales were poor and CBS' attitude became, if anything, even more negative. Not only was there no advertising to speak of but the publicity department was actually instructed to spend its time on anything *but* Bruce and his album.

However, Bruce's corporate fans and friends came through for him, even when their efforts ran contrary to company policy. At that point one of the most instrumental figures was the head of CBS Publicity, Ron Oberman. He managed to balance the anti-Bruce directives with an inciteful strategy of his own, which ultimately benefited both Bruce's career and the coffers of his employers. Oberman understood that most critics don't want to be strong-armed or oversold but he also knew that Springsteen was bound to be a favorite with rock writers, many of whom had started out at the same time as Bruce in response to the very same music. And if Bruce's recorded output hadn't made it clear that he was the successor to the best and most positive aspects of the rock 'n' roll tradition, there was no doubt in Oberman's mind that his stage show would convince anyone. So he discreetly sent out Bruce's albums, with the suggestion that he would make arrangements for any interested party to see Bruce perform.

And perform he did, though there were a few changes he finally had to face. One of the most serious problems with the early band was Mad Dog Lopez' inconsistent drumming. He and Bruce went so far back together that the decision to let him go was a difficult one, but it was finally made, and David Sancious recruited his friend Ernest 'Boom' Carter to fill the gap. If nothing else, this made for an interesting stage show, and with Bruce fronting a predominantly black band, he'd often get into a jive-ass funky mood and even took to wearing baggy pants. But this line-up was short lived since Sancious was offered a recording contract with Epic Records which he felt compelled to accept. He also took Boom with him, but not before some work had begun on the next album. CBS again tried to convince Bruce to use session players to fill the gaps, and in fact he did bring in a few horn players to flesh out parts of *Born To Run*, but he wanted permanent band members, not only for the cohesion and creative contributions, but for the all important stage shows. Bruce discussed his opinions on this score quite frankly. 'I don't hire studio musicians. I don't want guys with big houses playing for me. I just put an ad in the paper and people come out and play. You take a kid off the street and he'll play his heart out for you. If someone's primarily interested in how much money he's going to make, I don't want him playing for me.'

As it turns out, Springsteen did put an ad in the paper (The Village Voice) and though he didn't exactly get kids, he didn't get people who were primarily in it for the money either, since as Bruce told it, 'I've got some great musicians in my band, and I'm payin' 'em terrible money. I pay myself the same, but it's terrible for me too. I mean, we're barely makin' a livin' scrapin' by.' But with the mere mention they were looking for a drummer and keyboard player, the calls flooded in. Not all were auditioned, but the two new members must have been obvious choices. They had both just been working in the orchestra pits of Broadway musicals and their theatrical experience stood them in good stead for the performance challenge of working with Bruce.

The drummer chosen was Max Weinberg, soon dubbed 'Mighty Max', who was as strong as he was solid and who possessed the added appeal of having come from New Jersey to study with the legendary Bernard Purdie. The other addition was Roy Bittan, and though some people claim that he entered the band after sitting in during a Boston show, the main point is that he's in and his playing has become ever more integral to the sound. Bittan was soon recognized as the foremost musician in the band and for reasons that may have to do with his hairline, his temperament, Professor Longhair, or perhaps real scholarliness, he was ceremoniously renamed 'The Professor'. Bittan hailed from Far Rockaway, New York, and while it isn't Jersey, it's the closest thing to the Shore that N.Y.C. has to offer. Once the band was together it should have

been a fairly short sprint through the recording studio, but there were some major artistic issues still unresolved.

By the spring of '74 Bruce had written some material that would end up on *Born To Run* — most notably the title track — but, for a combination of reasons he was having trouble getting a handle on his material. Partly it was a matter of perfecting his songwriting and fine tuning his vision, but there was also the crucial matter of production which had hampered his efforts thus far. There was also a third and more subtle dilemma — the pressure on him associated with an artist's third album being the mythical 'make it or break it' release. Superficially Bruce was in control and though there was a lot of wisdom in his comments, his understanding didn't make him immune to the ever mounting pressure for a new and GREAT album. So Bruce declared, 'When it's ready, it'll be there. I can't be pressured. I decided a long time ago, I know who I am and where I come from. And I know what it is to be caught up in the pressure. You start thinking that you're something else.

You start becoming a product of the entertainment business. I try to keep my perspective on the thing. It's even for the good of the record company that I do that, because I'll give them my best and it'll work out for the best in the end.'

Despite the strength and near revolutionary quality of his stand, he was sorely in need of some guidance, and it came unexpectedly in the form of Jon Landau. Landau at that time was in charge of the record review section of Rolling Stone magazine, and also wrote a column for The Real Paper in his home town of Boston. For a fairly young critic, Landau had impressive credentials, with production credits (on the MC5's *Back In The U.S.A.* and two for Livingston Taylor) and a fairly heavy reputation in musical/critical circles. He'd been hearing raves from both CBS and various Rolling Stone writers, and although he hadn't checked out Springsteen live, he decided to review *The Wild, The Innocent And The E Street Shuffle* in the Real Paper the week before one of Bruce's Boston shows.

*The* archtypal Bruce picture

What developed into a major relationship can be said to have really started there, because in his article Landau offered exactly the kind of particular criticism and specific encouragement that Bruce needed. He pointed out both Lopez' weak drumming and the production flaws that plagued the previous album, but he also called E Street a major work. After recommending that Springsteen get the production up to spec and 'just throw some more hot ones on the vinyl', he predicted that with the ride Bruce was offering, it was just a matter of time before he started picking up passengers. Acting on his own advice, Landau went down to see Springsteen's benefit show for friend and club owner Joe Spadafora at Charley's in Boston.

As Landau walked up, he caught sight of Springsteen bouncing on his toes in the cold, reading his review which was posted in the club window. After asking if he thought the piece was good to which Bruce replied, 'It's good, I've read better, you know', Landau introduced himself and the two went inside. There Landau had a little more explaining to do for Mike Appel who rather defensively started the conversation with 'So you don't like the album's production, huh?' That evening's performance together with another a month later inspired Landau to write an article which had repercussions that are felt to this day. Beginning on a personal note about how it was four a.m., raining and he'd just turned twenty-seven that night, Landau reiterated what rock 'n' roll had meant to him and how that initial spark and spirit had been all but buried. He then turned his attention to Bruce and the future saying, 'But tonight there is someone I can write of the way I used to write, without reservations of any kind. Last Thursday at Harvard Square Theatre, I saw my rock 'n' roll past flash before my eyes. And I saw something else: I saw rock 'n' roll's future and its name is Bruce Springsteen. And on a night when I needed to feel young again, he made me feel like I was hearing music for the first time.'

The article continued for another paragraph, but it was the dramatic line about rock 'n' roll's future that caught everyone's eye. The most immediate effect was that CBS gobbled it up and put it on every piece of Bruce related advertising. Combined with other reviews inspired by Landau's piece, the quote as ad copy did the trick and E Street and Greetings actually began to show up in the charts. This immediately took some pressure off Bruce but in the long run it only increased the expectations for his next album. Dave Marsh made the point that a partisan review (especially about a previously underrated artist or work) coming from a highly respected writer raises the whole level of criticism on the subject. As Marsh put it, the question would no longer be 'is he good?' but 'is he great?', and the same criterion would apply to his music. Bruce didn't really appreciate Columbia's capitalization on the quote, saying that it was 'a very personal thing', but it was also a shot in the arm because 'it came at a time when a lot of people — including the record company — were wondering whether I really had it. It gave me a lot of hope. Landau's quote helped me reaffirm a belief in myself. The band and I were making $50 a week. It helped me go on. I realized I was gettin' through to somebody.'

Bruce got in touch with Landau to thank him for the rave, and in the process established the foundations of their relationship. Landau took the time to answer Bruce's questions about the possible functions of a producer, while also demonstrating a knowledge of the machinations of the music business that were still outside of Bruce's experience. Thus Landau became a friend and mentor, and with his critical background, he was invaluable in advancing Bruce's education in both technical and aesthetic matters.

After a good beginning, Bruce was back at 914 to record Born To Run, and Landau was in the hospital for an operation to cure an intestinal disorder. He then went through a period of convalescence and a divorce, after which he decided to move back to New York where he and Bruce rekindled their friendship. This was in November of '74, and it was none too soon for Bruce, who'd managed to record Born To Run, but which again was just a bit too long for standard A.M. programming formats. Mike Appel was impatient and also confident that the rest of the record would follow swiftly — so he took the liberty of releasing tape copies to friendly disc jockeys. The result was two underground hits (the other song was The Fever) and some problems. CBS was incensed because it had sure hits but no records to sell, and they thought that an exclusive relationship with certain DJs would cause problems with other stations when the record did come out; there was a possibility that they might not play it if they felt slighted. In Appel's defense, he was only repaying loyalty, since people like Kid Leo in Cleveland and Ed Sciaky in Philly had been playing and promoting Springsteen all along. The fact that half the initial pressing of E Street had sold in Philadelphia could be attributed in part to Bruce's live shows, but Sciaky's enthusiasm was certainly a factor. Like Appel, he was a zealot for Bruce, asking first time concert goers if they were prepared to accept Bruce as their personal savior, and so on. In any case, the problems might not have grown so out of proportion if a record had been forthcoming, but Bruce showed no signs of settling for less than perfection or to die trying.

So when Landau came to town, Bruce already had demos of several songs to play for him including Backstreets, Jungleland and Born To Run. They were the hot ones Landau had been talking about, and he did what he could to point out production problems, as well as suggesting some arrangement changes. Bruce was fast becoming addicted to Landau's objectivity and clarity, a situation which Paul Nelson of the Village Voice summarized quite clearly: 'If Landau was somewhat in awe of the kind of instinctual genius who could resolve aesthetic problems by compounding them, Bruce had no less respect for someone who invariably got to ten by counting out nine individual numbers, one at a time. It was the ideal marriage of creative madness with controlling method.' This ideal marriage began as a friendship and developed into a professional relationship, since Bruce began inviting Landau to various recordings, mixing and rehearsal sessions, where it also became apparent to the band that Landau had some positive criticism and suggestions. Appel was less than delighted with the competition and an early suggestion by Bruce to have Landau join the production team was rejected as unworkable. However, after Landau helped restructure *Thunder Road* and trimmed the tune from seven minutes to nearly four, Bruce put his foot down and Landau became an official co-producer. (The original pressing of the LP carried a sticker which specified that *Born To Run* was produced *only* by Appel and Bruce, where as the rest of the album is credited to all three. It's not difficult to figure out who wanted the distinction made.)

All the problems were not immediately resolved, but to aid the sound quality Landau moved the band into a top flight New York Studio and signed on a great young engineer by the name of Jimmy Iovine. Iovine was adept at getting the so-called 'block sound' which avoided needless track separation, and gave the production a full, dense sound which was the modern equivalent of Phil Spector's 'wall of sound'. The basic tracks were laid down quickly, but Bruce then spent months agonizing over the lyrics of several tunes, with Landau again offering advice. But there were times when even he couldn't move Bruce and, as a consequence, most of the summer was spent camped out at the studio with Bruce poring over minute details. Fortunately the band members had total confidence in Bruce and were prepared to be there for him to work out all the songs that never made it on the album (of which *The Fever* is just one example) and to endlessly rework the material.

It was during these sessions that one of the stalwarts of the E Street Band came fully on board; while recording the horn parts to *Tenth Avenue Freeze Out*, Miami Steve Van Zandt was ushered into the big time. With several high paid horn players on hand there was general dissatisfaction with the mousy arrangement that had been previously worked out. Steve's R&B experience was called on, and his solution was so true to character that he suddenly became personally and professionally irresistible. He walked into the studio and told New York's top players 'Okay boys, put those charts away' and proceeded to *sing* them their lines. That was just what Bruce wanted and Steve was immediately put on the payroll. Such triumphs were balanced by the tribulations of a record that 'wanted everything' from everybody. The entire production team had given the album all they had for months, but for Bruce it had been more like a year. In the end he was reluctant to let go of his obsession, and this was exemplified in his attitude towards the approval of the master disc. It is the last step over which the artist has much control and he consequently rejected several masters for assorted reasons, soon getting so frustrated that he threw one out of a window and was ready to do the same with another which the band received on the road and had to listen to on an $89 stereo. Due to low fidelity and fading objectivity, he decided he hated the whole thing, was going to scrap the album and release live recordings instead. When Landau heard about this lunacy he again had to give Bruce a dose of perspective, reportedly saying something to the effect of 'Look, you're not supposed to like it. You think Chuck Berry sits around listening to *Maybellene*? And when he does hear it, don't you think he wishes a few things could be changed?' Bruce

could accept that logic, and exhausted, he allowed the record to be released.

With the possible exception of Bruce, everyone who heard *Born To Run* knew that it fulfilled all of Landau's predictions; that it was an instant classic and the hottest rock 'n' roll album of the decade. As the tapes made their way around CBS, past disagreements dissolved and it was decided to launch an all out publicity campaign in conjunction with the LP. Bruce already had a tremendous cult following in certain areas, but the rest of the world was largely unprepared for Springsteen's emergence. Through a combination of Appel's publicity strategy and CBS' marketing efforts, Springsteen and his music appeared to spring full blown out of nowhere. This was obviously not the case, and Clarence Clemon's response to suggestions that Bruce and the band were overnight sensations was to ask people where *they'd* been. Once Appel realized they had a hit on their hands, he decided that he wouldn't grant any interviews unless Bruce was guaranteed a cover story. Had the critical groundswell not turned into a flood in the wake of Jon Landau's article, Appel might not have been asked for *any* interviews, but the waves of criticism crested in a piece by Henry Edwards, New York Times Critic at Large, who nearly topped Landau by titling his piece, 'If There Hadn't Been A Bruce Springsteen, Then The Critics Would Have Made Him Up'. The article was fairly cynical, with Edwards claiming that Bruce was derivative and so on — but it was considered significant just by virtue of appearing in the Sunday Times. This attention to Bruce created a buzz in the media which led to decisions by both Time and Newsweek to do cover stories on Bruce for the same week. Newsweek called its piece 'The Making Of A Rock Star', though they were offbase in their premise that Bruce's popularity was the result of hype. Time on the other hand knew about the Newsweek story, and motivated by a sympathetic journalist named Jay Cocks, concentrated instead on what made Bruce important to his fans. Needless to say, when both magazines appeared on October 27, 1975 with Bruce's face on the covers, he suddenly became someone to be reckoned with. Bruce's tendency was to ask 'Why should I be on the cover of Newsweek? I don't deserve it. That's for Presidents.' His father had a better point: 'Better you than *another* picture of the President?'

Both Time and Newsweek made mention of the sorry state of rock, and Mike Appel in typical fashion hit the nail on the head when he told the Newsweek writers that 'the industry is at the bottom of the barrel. We've got people scratching around looking for new talent. There's an amazing paucity of talent because there hasn't been anyone isolated enough to create a distinctive point of view. What I'm waiting for, what Bruce Springsteen is waiting for, and we're all waiting for is something that makes you want to dance. Something we haven't had for seven or eight years. Today anything remotely bizarre is gobbled up as the next big thing. What you've got to do is get the universal factors, to get people to move in the same three or four chords. It's the real thing! Look up America! Look up America! — And people did.

While at the time Bruce didn't believe that all of this would sell records, he later realized that perhaps it had gotten a few more people to the shows and stores. The response to the live shows was suddenly tremendous, helped again by the airplay, and backed up by the critics, all of which was reinforced by one of Mike Appel's best ever publicity moves. Thinking big as usual, Appel wanted to book Madison Square Garden to announce Bruce's arrival but he was finally convinced that it was out of the question. Instead they booked The Bottom Line on West 4th St for ten shows over five nights. Of the four thousand seats available, over nine hundred were purchased for promotion, and most journalists, rock writers and DJs of consequence were invited. Likewise, the fans turned up in droves — though many couldn't buy a seat — and one of the shows was broadcast live, resulting in one of the most famous Springsteen bootleg tapes. The shows were pheno-

menal and got better every night. So much was written that it would be difficult to choose the best reviews, though people like Dave Herman who'd resisted Bruce and CBS all along, went so far as to publicly apologize to his listeners and announce his conversion. Bruce claimed that the band walked into those gigs good and walked out great; 'they were down to intangibles.'

The Bottom Line shows have almost become myths both in terms of Bruce's career and as an experience for all who participated. They took place right after the release of his breakthrough album and in conjunction with all the publicity that attended it. They were also some of the last shows that Bruce would be able to do for such a small audience, at a time when all the distinctive elements of his stage show were intact. His raps and vamps may have been longer then, with more cover tunes in the set, but ever

since *Born To Run*, the demand has been for Bruce's own material. He already had songs like *Growin' Up*, *Blinded*, *Spirit In The Night*, *Rosalita* and *Jungleland* in his repertoire, but henceforth he wouldn't be able to get off the stage without performing most of *Born To Run*. And Clarence's sax contributions were so major and central to the band's sound and so rousing that the shows were a cross between a religious and a sexual experience; ie, the ultimate rock 'n' roll shows.

So we come to an album that in name alone conjures most major aspects of American teen/rock culture, with its similarity to the biker slogans 'Born To Die' and 'Born Losers' and its apparent reference to *Born To Be Wild*. Representing the synthesis of all these traditions, we are also confronted with Bruce Springsteen's vision of searching desperate youth in the form of *Born To Run*. The LP begins with *Thunder Road*, a song which one Asbury native claims takes its title from a real late night drag strip. The song certainly has that feel of acceleration to it, but with a story line similar to *Rosalita*. It starts in this place called Nowhere — which Bruce described as the setting for the album — with the singer catching a glimpse of Mary (every woman/every fan) dancing by herself on the porch. Referring to Roy Orbison 'singing for the lonely' (forgot to mention him as a key influence...), Bruce lays out another archetypal concern of his and the whole genre that he works in. It's about boy needing girl and girl needing boy. This recalls one comment Bruce made about his parents whom he considered to have 'a very deep love because they know and understand each other in a very realistic way'. It's that kind of unsentimental realism that allows Bruce to pull off a line like 'You ain't no beauty, but hey you're all right/Oh and that's all right with me.' He also tells her that 'I ain't no hero and that's understood', and all the redemption (another theme) he can offer is beneath a dirty hood. But the point is that he's there, he wants her and he wants her to show a little faith, take a risk and come with him to case the promised land. His promise is that 'all the promises will be broken' but those are assumed to be the promises made by and to others. There's metaphor on top of metaphor in this song (the religious language hints at more universal concerns) but one of the most interesting lines is the fairly simple invitation to take 'that long walk/From your front porch to my front seat' which objectively can't be very far, but the way Bruce stretches out the words and emphasizes them, it's like the decision to take those few steps will be the decision of a lifetime. He says he writes about critical moments, and for Mary this is one of them. He's offering freedom with the kind of boast that characterizes the album, 'It's a town full of losers and I'm pulling out of here to win'. The appeal of the road — whichever one you take — dominates this album, and though things are lost and found along the way, there is never any question that the traveling — the search — is necessary. If you're not looking, you'll never find anything.

The next song commences with somebody lost and alone in the city, along with simple but evocative imagery which conveys the whole feel of the night, where you can turn a corner and end up in a fall-out zone or a *Tenth*

*Avenue Freeze Out*. In the middle of the tale there's a leap, and suddenly from being in the position of trying to take 'all the heat they was givin'', the singer's gonna 'sit back right easy and laugh' 'cause now he's talking about his music and how when 'the Big Man joined the band/From the coastline to the city/All the little pretties raise their hands'. It's not the heaviest song on the album, but it's a nice salute to Clarence, 'The Big Man' — the horn parts sound great and the feeling is totally positive.

There's not a song on the album which if it begins in the daytime doesn't end up in the night, and some of the reasons for focusing on this time of day are laid out in *Night*. In Bruce's mind, and in most lives, things start 'when you get up every morning to the sound of a bell' and soon you 'get to work late and the boss man's giving you hell'. So what you live for and what feels right is to be 'out on a midnight run/Losing your heart to a beautiful one'. Bruce talked about how one of the concepts behind the LP was to do a guitar album, though he ended up writing most of the songs at the piano. This one is guitar all the way and Bruce shows his mastery of the instrument as the verses move back and forth between descriptions of how you work nine to five and somehow survive. 'Till the night' — at which point the music takes off with you. Along with the search for union ('And you'll find her somehow you swear') there's also the desire for a kind of escape as oblivion with the song ending on the line that 'You run sad and free/Until all you see is the night'. This song more than any other indicates the direction Bruce would take both thematically and musically with his next album.

*Backstreets* continues in a similar mood, though the story is quite different. It starts off with a friendship born 'one soft infested summer' when the singer and Terry were 'trying in vain to breath the fire we was born in'. The song could end after those lines, but it continues to chronicle the tale of two kids seeking solace with each other, hiding in the backstreets on nights when 'sometimes it seemed/you could hear the whole damn city crying'. The singer ends up crying too, because she leaves him, and it's inconceivable to him considering their bonds. A favorite line because it says so much about Springsteen's sensibility, sources and appeal is where he asks Terry to 'Remember all the movies, Terry/We'd go to see/Trying to learn to walk like the heroes we thought we had to be'. But the killer is that they eventually realize they're just like all the rest and all that remains is a search for something to blame to atone for their disappointments. The singer suggests that they 'Blame it on the lies that killed us/Blame it on the truth that ran us down'. This theme of lies, and dreams that are the product of lies, has dominated a good deal of Bruce's writing, and he's said that everyone knows the American Dream ain't about two cars in the garage but that 'it's about people loving and working together without steppin' on each other'. But he also knows that some poisonous aspects of the one dream keep the other from being lived, and it's for this reason that he finds his inspiration among the losers (the deluded or the cut-off) who are prisoners of their dreams. He takes them from dejection to defiance with the title track.

*Born To Run* was the first and most difficult song for Bruce to write, and though he didn't find a long term solution for the dilemma he poses, he offers a stance, a spirit and at least a direction. There's not a bad line in the song and most of them are great, clearly focusing on everything else that his music had dealt with thus far. David Sancious played on this tune and should get credit, but the real hero is Bruce as Brando who's again obsessed with walking in the sun. He lays out and what has to be escaped, and it's the world of Highway Nine and Jersey again. This song's got the extra speed and sleekness of a motorcycle, and Bruce (who's said on occasion that his *real* ambition in life is to be a lover) proves himself a master of eroticism when he tells Wendy that 'I want to guard your dreams and visions/Just wrap your legs round these velvet rims/And strap your hands across my engines'. The song continues with that edge of all or nothing because if you don't go for the whole deal you're either a huddling ghost or a broken hero. That feeling of last chance ('we gotta get out while we're young') pervades the song, and points again to the unity of this album where a song like this is made all the more poignant after the desertion of *Backstreets*. The togetherness is everything too, because he is just a 'scared and lonely rider' but if she believes that they'll 'get to that place' it almost makes it possible. Until they get there the motto is 'tramps like us/Baby we were born to run' and like the last line of *Thunder Road*, it has literally given an impetus to many lives and made Bruce a true-life savior. (One writer has mentioned that Bruce had a poster of Peter Pan and Wendy in his room at this point, which may account for the name choice and provide a framework for the story.)

*She's The One* comes up next, and though musically it's as exciting as anything on the album, the lyrics are rather weak. In the song, Springsteen meets his match, even if the woman has a heart of stone. She's also 'got killer graces/And secret places/That no boy can fill' and the song is appropriately raucous as it celebrates this 'one'. There's a sudden and drastic change of mood into *Meeting Across The River* where only bass, piano, and faraway trumpet accompany the conversation between two small time hustlers heading into the city to make a deal. It shows Springsteen as a master story teller with an ability to paint a complete portrait in a very few lines, while his singing conveys all the desperation of the situation. The singer's got money problems and consequently 'Cherry's gonna walk', but if they can just find a ride and act tough ('Here stuff this in your pocket, it'll look like you're carrying a friend') then they'll be able to claim the two grand that's 'practically sitting here in my pocket'. The particular actions of the scene come alive and it's perfect down to the last detail because when he gets the money he isn't just gonna show it to Cherry, he's 'gonna throw that money on the bed'. Springsteen may be a romantic but he's aware of the real shit that happens in relationships and that's it. This song isn't performed, but its effect in the context of the album is to add to the overall narrative and it functions as dramatic aside.

Bruce seems quite familiar with the underworld of two-bit hustlers, and there are further hints of that world and its language in *Jungleland*. Again he is clearly mixing and overlaying metaphors, so words like 'connection' take on multiple meanings. But harkening back to *Incident On 57th Street*, *Jungleland* begins with a similar filmic motif of an outsider driving into the action, though this time the movement is from the opposite direction and the Magic Rat comes from Harlem (or the Bronx) to New Jersey. What he passes on arrival are 'barefoot girls sittin' on the hood of a Dodge, drinking warm beers in the soft summer rain', but as the song progresses the piano drops foreboding notes and the tension builds. From there it's roll up your pants and take a stab at romance until the symbol of repression in the form of the Maximum Lawmen comes to chase the kids down and it's time to take a stand. The image of the night world is amazing and complex, and Bruce describes it in the terms of his own theatrical style; 'There's an opera out on the Turnpike/There's a ballet being fought in the alley' and a rumble turns into a battle of the bands, with Bruce predicting the effect his music would have, where the 'hungry and the hunted' explode into rock 'n' roll bands (though sadly they're still 'hustling for the record machine'). All of the characters become increasingly desperate and while some dress in the 'latest rage' they're still defined by their loneliness and confusion. With his camera poised on the bedroom window Bruce has his (anti) hero walk away from his lover and go uptown where his 'own dream guns him down' and his death is only marked by his lover turning off her light. At this point the music builds dramatically and pulls together for the final lines which are the heart of the song. They also hint at why Bruce's contribution is so vital, because he was doing just what he sees *not* being done in the song. It's been pointed out that this is one of the earliest judgements made in a Springsteen song and, while it's significant that the album ends with a condemnation, it's not of the characters but of their situation: 'Outside the street's on fire/In a real death waltz/Between what's flesh and what's fantasy/And the poets down here/Don't write nothing at all/They just stand back and let it all be/And in the quick of a knife/They reach for their moment/And try to make an honest stand/But they wind up wounded/Not even dead/Tonight in Jungleland'. This still sounds as fresh in performance as the day it was written.

Bruce said what he had to say at that time, and it made him a hero. He brought back to the music world a spirit that most people had assumed was dead and buried, and in return he became the hero that he insisted he was not. He didn't make it easy for his new fans though, because not only was Bruce muted by the Maximum Law for some time, but when he came back his message wasn't a happy one. His statements were as strong as ever, but he wasn't about to offer false hopes or cheap exhilaration. As part of his 'give them more than they bargained for' philosophy, Bruce wanted things to be fun but knew that it was meaningless if it was easy too. Thus, the night time world was stripped of its Exxon signs and he took the journey to the darkness at the edge of town. Even the musical exuberance that had become an instant hallmark had to be toned down in sake of the message and mileau.

Bruce stares in amazement at the photographer in his kitchen

# SIX

# HELD UP WITHOUT A GUN

Before the full force of his success made itself felt, Bruce spoke about how 'all the stuff you dream about is there, but it gets diluted by all the other stuff that jumped on you by surprise'. One of the negative aspects of success is the lack of privacy and it would be a while before Bruce could sit back, since there was a long tour scheduled to back up the release of *Born To Run*. On the positive side, however, was the fact that more people were now making it to the shows, and the tour was an artistic success, though not a commercial one. This was partly due to Bruce's refusal to play the larger halls, and to the fact that he was now paying his band more, not to mention the myriad expenses of mounting a major rock tour. He was right to put on the best — albeit costly — show possible, since he was a hit everywhere he went. It was also an investment into what Bruce fully expected would be a long career.

He received his payoff right away with gigs like the Bottom Line shows, and one in New Jersey which was simply billed as 'Homecoming '75' — since everyone knew who was home. But in spite of all the triumphs, Bruce was evidently quite happy when the tour ended on New Year's Eve, allowing him to appraise his situation while the rest of the band took the time to work on other projects. Roy Bittan had been spotted by David Bowie and contributed to the *Station To Station* album, part of which was recorded in Philadelphia. Two of Bruce's tunes were recorded but not included in the final version, and Bruce even attended a couple of the sessions, reportedly traveling down from the Shore by bus. Jon Landau's reputation as a producer was now assured, and he went out to L.A. to begin work on Jackson Browne's *The Pretender*. Steve Van Zandt took on the production of his former band The Asbury Jukes' debut album, and Bruce made various contributions to that LP as well.

On the surface everything seemed fine, but Bruce soon had to grapple with problems on the business side of his career. Looking for some advice, he spoke to a fellow Jerseyite about what was on his mind. 'When all the attention started I was out in L.A. and Jack Nicholson came to a show. I asked him how he handled the attention.

He said for him, it was a long time coming and he was mostly glad to have it. I didn't quite see it that way. I bundled it all together into one general experience and labeled it 'bad'. I felt control over my life and career was slipping away and that all the attention was, like, an obstacle'. This makes sense coming from someone who likes to be anonymous when he chooses, and who enjoys slipping into the shadows — the source of some of his greatest inspiration. But, as he put it, 'after a while, I realized, well, time was on my side. Whatever happens, I wasn't gonna go away. I got no place to go.'

As it turns out, following a period of rest and relaxation, Bruce found that he couldn't go where he wanted to go, which was back to the recording studio. Instead, he wound up in court suing his manager. The entire story is fairly long and complicated, but there were two major factors which contributed to the split between Bruce and Mike Appel. The first and more personal element was the fact that Bruce was becoming more dependent on Jon Landau's advice and assistance and Appel resented the competition. Insult was added to injury when the Newsweek story featured a photo of Landau, Bruce and Karen Darbin and mistakenly referred to Landau as Bruce's manager. Through all of this, Bruce remained loyal to Appel, who was still carrying out most of the managerial functions, but when his contract came up for renewal Bruce finally realized what kind of agreement he'd signed. Even forgetting about the paltry royalty percentage he received and the fact that he'd gotten only one accounting statement in four years, or even that Appel had failed to pay his taxes for three of the four years, what finally got to Bruce was the realization that he didn't own the songs he'd written. Bruce later explained that 'I didn't know what publishing *was*. You're gonna think it's what happens to books. It's one of those words.' What the word meant in his case was that since Appel owned the publishing rights, in effect he owned the songs. Bruce didn't want to be forced into a legal battle since he'd always liked Appel and felt that the others just didn't understand him. Bruce could forgive almost anything, until it involved control of his music. As he later described it: 'he (Appel) worked hard for a long time — we all worked hard — and he sacrificed and OK, he deserved something for it. But what I wanted was the thing itself: my songs. It got so where, if I wrote a book, I couldn't even quote my lyrics — I couldn't quote *Born To Run*! That whole period of my life just seemed to be slipping out of my hands. That's why I started playing music in the first place — to control my life. No way was I gonna let that get away.'

So what ensued was a year long legal battle in which Bruce originally sued Appel for breach of fiduciary trust. This trust implies working in the client's best interest, but due to the conflicts inherent in being manager, producer and publisher, as well as attempting to become the booking agent, and with blatant mis-handling of finances on top of that, Bruce's point was that Appel had betrayed his agreement. Appel then countered with a restraining order which kept Bruce and Landau from entering a recording studio together. He also tried to attach Bruce's box office receipts, thereby forcing him into a settlement on the grounds of economic necessity, since Laurel Canyon was in possession of almost all the money earned in Bruce's name. Initially, the case went in Appel's favor and, because Bruce was intent on working with Landau as his producer, no new album was forthcoming. However, the band did manage to tour and those shows gave Bruce the money and the encouragement to keep up the fight. The details of the settlement have never been made public but in the end Bruce and his lawyers were able to effect a turnaround and the management contract was legally severed. He was still bound though, by the terms of the original contract and thus did not end up with possession of the publishing rights to his songs. But Bruce was right in seeing that time was on his side, and finally in 1982 he was able to buy the rights back from Laurel Canyon.

The whole process took its toll on Bruce, but he survived and stated afterwards that 'I'm more alive than I ever was, and *that* is the story.' Part of that story was written into *Darkness On The Edge Of Town*. By the time the record came out in '78, Bruce had this to say. 'I had a big awakening in the past two, three years. Much bigger than people would think. Learned a lot of things, saw a lot of things. Realized a lot of things about my own past. So it's there on the record.'

Springsteen has been consistently described as class-conscious, which is notable not because he's more class-conscious than many other artists (consider Duran Duran or Bowie), but because he is focussed on the class which he springs from, continues to ally with, and attempts to both represent and entertain. This class-consciousness is an element in all of his work, but in *Darkness* it is primary. Because of this orientation, many found it oppressive, but it's *about* oppression, and in the best cases Bruce either bares it, faces it, or beats it back. As usual there are a couple of lighter weight cuts, but the general strengths of Springsteen's vision more than make up for these weaknesses.

He worked on the *Darkness* album for almost a year, not to mention all the thinking and writing that went on prior to production and, by the time he was finished, he had again forged a unique vision as well as band and vocal sound. The basic message here is what also pervaded his subsequent work, with variations in emphasis and theme. And it's not *about* cars and escape as many seem to think, but rather, as *Darkness* makes clear, it's about the need for constant struggle and the need to face things rather than escape from them. These ideas were a product of Springsteen's own recent experiences, and they were honed under Landau's tutelage.

Landau's influence on this LP is tangible, ranging from his preferred dense sound to encouraging Bruce's study of film and literature. With Landau's encouragement Bruce came to see himself as a genre artist in the manner of a Sergio Leone, a John Ford or a Flannery O'Connor, whose characters and situations are perpetually re-explored. Another unique element of Springsteen's music is that it progresses through time, with the main character being roughly the same age as the songwriter. He hints at this while speaking more generally about the differences between the albums.

According to Bruce, *E Street* was warm and had a sort of 'in-society, group involvement' feeling to it, whereas on *Born To Run* 'it sort of gets down to usually a guy and a girl. And for me *Born To Run* maintains some warmth, but there was a certain element, a certain fear that starts to come in. I don't know why. And on this record (*Darkness*), I think it's less romantic — it's got more, a little more, isolation. It's sort of like I said, "Well, listen, I'm twenty-eight years old and the people in the album are around my age." I perceive 'em to be that old. And they don't know what to do... There's less of a sense of a free ride than there is on *Born To Run*. There's more a sense of: if you wanna ride, you're gonna pay. And you'd better keep riding.'

This sense of things is reflected in almost every song on the album and every statement Springsteen made about it. He's no politician. He doesn't tell you *what* to do or exactly *how* to wage your fight, but he always emphasizes the struggle itself, and has found a lot of subtle ways to tell his listeners about the price you pay for fighting, and the even higher price of surrender.

Beginning the album with *Badlands*, the basic subjects are laid out, as are Bruce's attitudes. Talking about how he's 'caught in a crossfire/That I just don't understand', certain things stand out crystal clear. In words that could be applied to art, love, politics, you name it, Springsteen states that 'I don't give a damn, for the just in-betweens/Honey I want the heart, I want the soul, I want control/Right now'. He sings about the necessity of having a dream and trying to make it real because otherwise you 'Spend your life waiting/For a moment that just don't come/Well, don't waste your time waiting'. All sorts of advice for survival is offered, like letting the broken hearts stand as part of the price you've got to pay, because the main thrust should be in the effort to 'keep pushin' till it's understood and these badlands start treating us good.' The song is addressed to those with a notion deep inside, that it ain't no sin to be glad you're alive, and though that notion's sometimes buried pretty deep, without that spark of life Bruce knows that it's impossible to get through. He does create a few characters

New Years Eve 1978/9 in Cleveland Ohio – and the rare sight of Bruce with a bottle in his hand

who are that far gone, though they're not generally sympathetic.

Springsteen in conversation is like Springsteen the song-writer, he tells parable-like tales, altering the versions slightly and stringing them together in different combinations. What follows is a fairly long quote which included a few stories he was using at the time to illustrate his concerns. 'You grow up and they bury you' he begins, talking about how pretty soon you're six, maybe twelve feet under, and *maybe* by some grace or method you finally get one hand free. And maybe you don't. 'That's what I'm talking about. That some people get dug in so deep that there's a point where it stops getting on them and they roll over, start digging down. Because they don't know which way is up. You don't know if you're digging sideways, up, down, you don't *know*...until something comes along, if you're lucky, and shakes you 'til all of a sudden you have a certain sense of direction and at least know where you're going. A lot of people don't ever get to that. You go into bars and you see the guys wandering around in there who got the crazy eyes. They just *hate*. They're looking for an immediate expenditure of all this build-up. They're just *screaming* to throw it all off. But you can't and it turns into, like, death throes. A guy walks into a bar, a little guy, and he walks up to another guy, a *dome*, and the little guy's looking to get *creamed*. Looking to get massacred. He *wants* to. "Look", he's saying. "I'm dying here and I don't know what the fuck to do". It's a scary thing when you see the guys that ain't gonna get out. You just see too many faces. It's the kind of thing where you can't save everybody, but you gotta try.'

So with this album Bruce became a man with a mission, and what he has to say is presented in more direct fashion than usual. He took material based on his own life and experiences, tied them into universal themes, and added his own poetry and interpretation. Such is the case with his flaming version of *Adam Raised A Cain* which begins sounding a lot like *The Fever*, a classic Springsteen tune that was also written during this period. The use of religious themes and language on this LP is slightly ironic, since Bruce rejected Catholicism at a fairly early age. It was replaced by his own fairly stringent moral code and philosophy but is expressed in the same religious terms. Using the story of Adam, Cain and Abel as a starting point (evidently inspired by use of the same in *East Of Eden*) Bruce spins a tale about recognizing who, what and why you are — others 'fit you with position', but your mother calls you by your 'true name'. The singer and his father have 'the same hot blood burning in our veins' and the coming to terms doesn't end because 'you know it's never over, it's relentless as the rain'. This song clarifies one of Bruce's obsessions, the personal significance of what kind of life you're born into. In the final lines he makes a strong statement about all of this: 'You're born into this life paying/For the sins of somebody else's past/Daddy worked his whole life/For nothing but the pain/Now he walks these empty rooms/Looking for something to blame/You inherit the sins/You inherit the flames/Adam raised a Cain'. At about the same time Bruce wrote another father/son song but he held it over for the next chapter and *Independence Day* appears on *The River*. (*The Promise* had also been a favorite with fans during his 'lawsuit tour', but since it was usually interpreted as relating directly to his suit with Appel, he decided not to include it.)

The next song on the album is *Something In The Night* and, like *Factory*, it's one of Bruce's denser songs literally weighted by the dragging drum thud. (In retrospect Weinberg thought it heavy-handed.) It's a song about defeat, of someone on their last go 'round, 'when nothing is forgotten or forgiven and things can't be lived down'. Not only does this one recall the driver in *Night*, but also part of a rap Bruce used to introduce *Thunder Road*. He talked about how out in the middle of the desert there was a notice with a picture of Geronimo on it pointing to a small dirt road which stated that this was the land of 'peace, love, justice, and *no mercy*'. No one gets any mercy on this record and that fact prompted Bruce to consider calling it *American Madness*. The song also contains a first reference to what has become a symbolic border: the state line. Sometimes it gets crossed, and sometimes, as in this number, it doesn't.

The people on this album are all looking for something and have to pass through various stages and obstacles if they're to find what they seek. In the beginning of the next song the singer must travel through the darkness of Candy's hall to get to *Candy's Room*. The reason for traveling through the darkness is to find 'hidden worlds that shine', and those things are love and truth. Generally this is one of the lighter songs on the LP, but there's something to be learned from why a girl like Candy (with fancy clothes and diamond rings) would fall for the singer. It's because 'She knows that I'd give all that I got to give', which pretty much sums up Springsteen's ideal for living and loving.

*Racing In The Streets* is the first song to take drag racing and make it part of the narrative, but again the song is more involved than its superficial subject. It amounts to a Bruce remake of the classic *Dancing In The Streets*, and though *Racing* doesn't have the same easy optimism as the Martha and The Vandellas' song, it has the same upward thrust. The main character is a fighter, and though he starts off sounding tired and down, he talks about how 'Some guys they just give up living/And start dying little by little, piece by piece/Some guys they come home from work and wash up/And go racing in the street'. He's one that goes racing. The narrative is complex, ranging over time and several subjects that are typical of Springsteen's work, but one that gets a lot of attention on this album and more on the next, is the theme of people who've given up and so have nothing to live for. This is the case with his girl, whom he 'won' by being the baddest guy on the strip, but that was three years ago and 'now there's wrinkles around my baby's eyes' which wouldn't be so bad were it not for the fact that they've also become the 'eyes of one who hates for just being born'. The solution that he finds is that they're gonna ride to the sea and 'wash these sins off our hands' and so a symbolic order is established which carries through to *The River*. If Marley hadn't used the title, perhaps Bruce could have called these *Redemption Songs*.

The *Promised Land* that the last couple rumbled

through is Chuck Berry's euphemism for America (and Springsteen's for what should be but isn't) and it's the title of the next track. *Promised Land* echoes *Badlands* in several ways, and the essence of the song is that same effort to 'take one moment into my hands'. These songs are about people with no personal power, so everything remains an unfulfilled promise. He swears he's tried to 'live the right way' (which he defines by the fact that 'I get up every morning and go to work each day'), but realizes that your eyes go blind and your blood runs cold, until he again is describing that same need to explode. The line about how he wants to 'take a knife and cut this pain from my heart/Find somebody itching for something to start' hints at themes in both *I'm On Fire* and *Dancing In The Dark*. These albums have a thematic resemblance, though the desperate intensity of *Darkness* makes it resemble *Nebraska* more in feeling. As usual, things are laid out clearly in the final verse, and Bruce's singing of this part makes it one of the high points of the album. The singer sees a dark

cloud rising from the desert floor and he decides to head straight into it. It's 'gonna be a twister to blow everything down/That ain't got the faith to stand its ground'. It's significant that he welcomes it and there's little doubt that he will survive.

The next song is purely about survival. *Factory* hardly moves at all, and in that sense the music is a perfect complement to the lyrics. The feeling of drudgery in the chorus ('It's the working life, the working, just the working life') will stick with you, along with the image of the 'end of the day, factory whistle cries/Men walk through these gates with death in their eyes.' (That death will kill, as *Nebraska* proves.)

From here on out it just gets heavier and though there's still the impulse to break away, the singer is now surrounded by his own demons in the form of 'weak lies and cold walls' and he makes the choice to walk alone and out into *Streets Of Fire*. The last few lines describe choosing a certain kind of voluntary withdrawal but which is almost

song is also quite romantic in its desperate way; not everyone meets their lover in 'the field behind the dynamos'.

*Darkness On The Edge Of Town* begins with the explanation that the woman of the singer's dreams never had 'that' blood burning in her veins. Now she lives in Fairview with a style she's trying to maintain, while he, in contrast, is concerned with exposing that emptiness in favor of truth. Unlike the character in *Badlands*, he's not gonna spit in anybody's face, he's gonna go it alone without recrimination because he has to, and because he can't do any less than what he knows. In this piece, the singer conveys his awareness to Sonny (who was also his partner in *Racing In The Streets*) and he tells him. 'Everybody's got a secret Sonny/Something they just can't face/Some folks spend their whole lives trying to keep it/They carry it with them every step they take'. He then explains why you can find everything on the edge. It's because people keep going 'til some day, they just cut it loose/Cut it loose or let it drag them down/Where no one asks any questions, or looks too long in your face/In the darkness on the edge of town'. Bruce himself was searching for those proverbial 'things that can only be found in the darkness on the edge of town'. When he spoke about making the album he talked about how with Landau's help 'little consciousness barriers were dropping' and he set out to effect the same thing in his listeners. It's not an easy listen, 'cause he can only hint at the secrets of his characters and their worlds, but it's well worth peering into those shadows for the other side of the story and glimpses of 'hidden world's that shine'.

(During the long recording process and year of legal battles, Springsteen's songs were brought before the public more and more frequently by other artists. If he had not already recorded a tune, he would rarely bother to put it on vinyl, which is the case with *The Fever*, given to Southside Johnny and *Fire*, which went to Robert Gordon. *Because The Night* was another composition which became Patti Smith's only major hit single. (Bruce does perform his version sometimes but with slightly different lyrics.) This collaboration came about during the long encampment in The Record Plant, where Jimmy Iovine, who was also producing Patti, came to Bruce requesting something that would furnish the hit she so badly needed at that point. The result of Bruce's music and her rewrite did the trick, and also produced some fine photos of the two Jersey kids, one who'd been raised 'talkin' about William Burroughs' but who needed Bruce's touch to reach a broad audience. Greg Kihn also covered *For You*, The Hollies tried *Sandy* and Manfred Mann did his own version of *Spirit In The Night* and *Blinded By The Light*, which also resulted in top British sales. After *Born To Run* Bruce was also introduced to his idol Phil Spector, and later met Phil's ex-wife, Ronnie Spector. He gave Ronnie a song, she gave him a kiss and a poster of herself which is said to be a prized possession. In the meantime, the likes of X's John Doe performed 'risky material' like *Born To Run* in the bars of Baltimore and Cleveland and Frankie Goes To Hollywood recently covered the same tune for their *Welcome To The Pleasuredome* LP.)

forced on the singer by his awareness of the world he's inhabiting. Bruce has compared his pen to a film camera with which he'll zoom in on characters for a small moment, explore rather than resolve. Viewed in this light, the lines 'I live now, only live with strangers/I talk to only strangers/I walk with angels that have no place' might be seen as an extreme point from which he will begin his return to humanity. The pain in Bruce's voice as he sings this defies description.

*Prove It All Night* is another Bruce classic and it amounts to a lot more than a clichéd adolescent sexual challenge. When the singer tells the girl 'you want it, you take it, you pay the price', he's talking about *everything*. Like the previous song in which the characters have to appraise themselves and their relationship to the world honestly, he's willing to take her to the extremes where such knowledge resides, where she'll learn 'what it means to steal, to cheat, to lie/What it's like to live and die'. The

# SEVEN

# INDEPENDENCE DAY

Having survived the long wait for *Darkness*, which was devoured and went platinum immediately, Bruce's fans were slightly more prepared for the lengthy gap before his next release. And, while no one was surprised by its excellence, he again confounded most expectations. Jon Landau was quoted as saying that 'Bruce is determined before he dies to make the greatest rock 'n' roll record ever'. In retrospect, *The River* was just one large step towards achieving that goal, but since *Nebraska* and *Born In The U.S.A.* didn't yet exist, people could be excused for thinking that *The River* was that record. Again the album was a kind of summation of the best that Springsteen had yet written, sung, played and heard, and as usual contained some seeds of what would follow.

Bruce moved outside of his own experience here, concentrating on developing his characters and advancing their stories. In this fictional narrative he again proved himself to be an inciteful and sensitive observer whilst becoming more economical with words. Each tale is now tightly focussed on a particular theme, while his use of appropriate detail gives the 'real' and 'everyday' texture he sought. There was also the extra treat of two albums' worth of music which existed as a unified whole, allowing him to advance and examine the characters from several angles. Although many of Bruce's concerns are reflected in his songs not everything can be expressed that way. Thus interviews are helpful in order to get a greater insight into a man whose power Peter Knoebler described as 'always having been that he writes what he knows, and that he's in touch with it, that he makes you feel it too.' Bruce confirms 'I stick too close to the other side to know what's real about this side (the life of a rock star). And I still got too many people who are close to me who are still living on that other side.' This desire to stay in touch with 'the other side' is why he continues to live in Jersey and is in contact with the likes of Vietnam Vet Mike Kovaks, whose book about his experience in Vietnam inspired Bruce to do one of his few benefit concerts.

*The River* is an album obsessed with love and marriage, in this case among the American lower-classes. Bruce himself is still unmarried but this has no bearing on his ability to observe others. He sees marriage or mating as a natural part of growing older and, as usual, the characters in the songs have all aged a couple of years along with Bruce.

On the subject of moving onward, it was on this record that Bruce clearly started to move beyond the limits of the rock genre. It's one of the generic pecularities of most rock music that its subjects rarely move beyond adolescence. Bruce understands this and has chosen to ignore this limitation, for which a great number of older rock fans are eternally grateful. As for the album's stylistic variations, Bruce has found room to move in other forms, though it seems unlikely that he will ever completely abandon rock. It has too much personal significance. As he put it: 'My whole life I was always around a lot of people whose lives just consisted of this compromising. They knew no other way — that's where rock 'n' roll became important because it said there could be'. At the same time he is concerned with those people who don't know any other way, which accounts for his attempt to reach them through different styles. He's talked about how 'I know what it's like not to be able to do what you want to do, 'cause when I go home that's what I see. It's no fun. It's no joke. I see my sister and her husband. They're living the lives of my parents in a certain kind of way. They got kids, they're working hard. They're just real nice, real soulful people. These are people you can see something in their eyes. It's really something. I know a lot of people back there.' He then goes on to quote his sister (the same comments are sometimes attributed to 'a friend'), and the essence of her statement forms the basis for the feeling and mood that is at the heart of the heavier songs on *The River*. Bruce said, 'I asked my sister, 'What do you do for fun?' 'I don't have any fun' she says. She wasn't kidding.'

Working on *The River* however was joyous, which made it a real departure from his previous LP. He had built, through strenuous effort, an audience, a band, a body of work and a firm business foundation, and he could 'sit back right easy and laugh'. He was too realistic to spend all his time laughing though, and the album maintained a

balance between the comic and the tragic that has always characterized his work.

There were a few problems surrounding *The River*, but they were minor compared to what he'd previously experienced. Nineteen seventy-nine started off in a slightly accident prone vein when a firecracker exploded just below Bruce's eye, thrown by a misguided fan. Later in the year, just after the band had moved into the Power Station to begin recording, Bruce had a motorcycle accident. This caused delays in recording as well as plenty of unsubstantiated rumors which turned a leg injury into spinal damage and included everything from love affairs to film offers.

But after his recuperation, and with a fair amount of material already written and tested on the *Darkness* tour, things seemed ready to fall into place. The production team was similar to the crew who'd worked on *Darkness*, though now Steve Van Zandt was officially a co-producer, as was the case with Landau's friend Chuck Plotkin who'd been called in to assist with the final mix on *Darkness*. Neil Dorfsman was chief engineer, while Jimmy Iovine and Bob Clearmountain did some recording and mixing for the 'hit' A.M. release cuts. Any delay in relation to *The River* was actually produced by Bruce's growing sense of giving the fans more than they might hope for, and his sense of responsibility in this regard was fostered in some odd ways.

While the album was being recorded, Bruce's DJ friend Carol Miller heard that New Jersey was looking for a state song, and got to work drafting and lobbying a bill that would make *Born To Run* that song. The bill was later changed to make the song the state's 'youth anthem', and she even tagged on a clause that would make Bruce the state's 'youth ambassador'. The bill went through but without the ambassador clause, although one New Jersey legislator remarked that Springsteen's endorsement could swing any election in the state. (Bruce has refrained from endorsements but this has not stopped several politicians from invoking his name.) George Kanzler of the Newark Star Ledger summed it up pretty well when he wrote about how much Bruce meant to the kids of Jersey. 'He's invested their commonplace lives, their Saturday night adventures, their teen rituals and reckless highway moments with all the significance of rock 'n' roll myth. He's not the only hero, they are too. Springsteen, with his music, has done more than any Chamber of Commerce or tourism promoter could do. He's made the Jersey shore musically important, nationally'.

It was these same kids who finally led Bruce in a direction he was inclined to take anyway. After months in the studio, Bruce was approached through some friends to perform at a couple of the MUSE (Musicians United For Safe Energy) concerts scheduled for Madison Square Garden in the fall of '79. He immediately said yes, which was surprising since that he doesn't generally publicly support political causes. He clearly supported the idea, however, especially in light of the disaster at nearby Three Mile Island in response to which he'd written in *Roulette*.

He let his music speak for him, but what spoke most clearly to Bruce was the audience's response to his shows,

where the fans were literally in a frenzy before he ever played a note. Kit Rachlis mentioned it in her review: 'The response Springsteen received as he walked onstage Friday night...was the most frenzied I'd ever heard. He was frightened, I suspect, but he never let it overwhelm him. Nor did he cut back; he simply made sure that it took him where he wanted to go.' This was also the case with the album, because after all those shows Bruce felt that a single album just wouldn't be enough for himself or for the fans. Besides, he had plenty of songs and his writing was still flowing. So they went back to the studio with the intention of creating a record as epic in length as it was in scope.

*The River* couldn't start off on a much better note than with the lively, Byrd-like, *Ties That Bind* which typically sets the theme for the rest of the album. As with many of the songs on this and previous albums, a woman is being addressed and she could be one of the characters from *Born To Run*, still misguided after *Darkness*, because as Bruce sees it, 'You're walkin' tough baby, but you're walkin' blind, to the ties that bind'. With one of his patented take-offs, Springsteen nods in the direction of country and western music which he was beginning to explore and here he refers to the Johnny Cash classic when he sings 'you walk cool, but darlin', can you walk the line (and face the ties that bind?)' After reiterating the impossibility of breaking those ties, the point is made that if the woman will just admit to the ties that bind her to the singer, there's the promise that 'We're runnin' now but darlin' we will stand in time/To face the ties that bind'. The point is made that you can't forsake the ties that bind you to humanity, though as Bruce demonstrates, there are all kinds of ties that bind, and while some should stand, some, like those in the song which follows, should be broken.

*Sherry Darling* is an amusing song and another early composition. This one tells an outrageous story of a guy driving his girlfriend's mother to the unemployment office for the umpteenth time and he's had it with her 'yappin' and 'big feet' not to mention the fact that 'there's girls melting out on the beach/And they're so fine but so out of reach/'Cause I'm stuck in traffic down here on 53rd St'.

The song goes on to chronicle how much fun he and Sherry could be having, with a totally raucous arrangement and with vocal contributions from everyone in the studio, but in relation to the 'ties that bind' theme, the point here is that 'Now Sherry my love for you is real/But I didn't count on this package deal/And baby this car just ain't big enough for her and me'. The question is, what's it gonna be?

From being trapped in traffic, Bruce gets more serious and portrays an insidious and menacing entrapment in a place he calls the *Jackson Cage*. The main character is a woman who's driving home 'into a row of houses/She just melts away/Like the scenery in another man's play'. She goes to a house where all the blinds are closed 'to keep from seeing things she don't wanna know', an attitude adopted by many of the female characters on this album. In fact, Springsteen was roundly criticized for his deprecating use of titles like 'darlin', 'baby' etc., and though his vision of most women's situations isn't a very happy one, it is largely realistic. Starting with cultural lock up at an early age, most people learn to put in their own blinders, 'till you become the hand that turns the key', and this is the trap that

Springsteen is consistently urging all of his characters to avoid. Sometimes Springsteen offers himself as a solution, but his real contribution here is in exposing the deadliness of the conditions under which most people live. There are plenty of disturbing images in the song but when he states that 'every day ends with wasted motion/Just crossed swords on the killing floor', he says plenty about the frustration and shackled potential of everyone that's been judged and handed life/Down in the Jackson Cage'. The prison imagery is powerful and towards the end the idea is developed that if this woman and the man who is her cell mate can raise each other up, perhaps there is some hope after all.

Returning to the theme of love, *Two Hearts* is one of the simplest songs on the album and exemplifies the directness, clarity and brevity that are manifest throughout the LP. The chorus more or less says it all: 'Two hearts are better than one/Two hearts can get the job done'. The presumption here is that 'the job' is any and all jobs, because as the singer admits 'Alone buddy there ain't no peace of mind/That's why I'll keep searching till I find my special one'.

ce and Roger Daltrey backstage at Madison Square Garden

What follows is one of the more obviously personal songs that Bruce has written, in which the singer is addressing his father, attempting a reconciliation with things that can't be fully reconciled on an emotional level. *Independence Day* draws together threads that have to do with America, its symbolic Independence Day on July 4th and, like *Sandy* (alias *4th Of July Asbury Park*), is set on the Jersey shore. The personal elements are clear to anyone with a knowledge of Bruce's background, with lines like 'the darkness in this house (and 'this town') has got the best of us' particularly standing out. The song is all about changes, which the singer takes some responsibility for, though only as the representative of what's new. He's got one foot firmly planted in his own past and the tradition which it represents, and a sympathy for it which has to be relinquished in the same way that he urges his father to 'say goodbye it's Independence Day'. But the issue is bigger than just the two of them, for 'it's Independence Day/All down the line'. This time however Bruce urges acceptance rather than the usual struggle. 'Well Papa go to bed now, it's getting late' and though he seems sad to see some things go, he realises change is essential and inevitable. One of the qualities which makes the song so powerful is its emotional honesty and true to life ambivalence when facing the fact that 'soon everything we've known will just be swept away'. This contradictory attitude is typical of Springsteen whenever he confronts tradition.

Side Two begins with the sparkling hit from the album but one that doesn't sit too easily with many a hardcore fan. Bob Clearmountain mixed the song to achieve a bright sound but it's so trebley that Bruce's voice is almost unrecognizable. Flo and Eddie (Mark Volman and Howard Kaylan) do the back-up vocals and you could be excused for thinking that one of them did the lead as well. They help give the song its pop sound, and it's only right that two guys who cancelled an L.A. show when they heard Bruce was playing because 'we'd rather see Bruce play than ourselves' should join him on a tune. *Hungry Heart* is slightly atypical because it's about somebody who broke the ties, who's 'Got a wife and kids in Baltimore Jack/I went out for a ride and I never went back', but at least he's realized that he's like 'a river that don't know where it's flowing/I took a wrong turn and I just kept going'. Likewise, the final line is true to theme; after saying that everybody needs a home and a place to rest, the singer claims that it 'Don't make no difference what nobody says/Ain't nobody like to be alone'. The problem is that sometimes a hungry heart can land you by yourself, as the last album made so clear.

*Out In The Street* could also have been on *Darkness*, with its talk of how good it feels to finally be your own man out in the street at the end of the work week. Bruce is jubilant in concert when he sings about being out where you can walk like you wanna walk and talk like you wanna talk, even though it's not perfect freedom since 'The black and whites cruise by/And they watch us from the corner of their eye'. Lyrically and musically the song harks back to *Friday On My Mind* by the Easybeats, which shows how wide ranging Springsteen's musical influences are and how well integrated into his songs.

An even livelier song follows, with a title that's such a common phrase that it seems inconceivable that no one's used it before. Springsteen's got a *Crush On You* and though it's not clear initially if it's on the car or the 'little stranger', 'She might be the talk of high society/She's probably got a lousy personality', and so it goes. Bruce goes crazy musing over this girl who could be anything from a Rockefeller to a bank teller, but he outdoes himself with pop culture references (and again on *I'm A Rocker*) saying that whoever she is she makes 'the Venus de Milo look like she's got no style' and that she makes 'Sheena of the Jungle look meek and mild'. It's too clever to be adolescent but also captures that girl-watching spirit perfectly, only to end with the boys laughing all the way down the street and warning 'watchout!'

The same 'watchout' is the message of *You Can Look (But You Better Not Touch)*, a warning which Bruce puts in two contexts. The first reference is to money-oriented property relations, summed up by the salesman's line, 'boy, you break that thing you bought it' with a humorous deep voice for the proper effect. On a larger level it's about the 'good things in life' which most of Bruce's characters rarely grasp and how the discrepancy between seeing and having can drive you mad. In the second verse the problem involves women and sex and includes the classic Bruce sentiment, 'she didn't get me excited she just made me feel mean'. Why? Because he turns on the TV and there's a pretty little girl who's wigglin' across the screen and she did what she shouldn't oughta, 'she looked straight into my eyes'. Since he can't get no satisfaction from her he calls Dirty Annie (Crazy Jane's cousin) and takes her to 'the drive-in just to get her alone'. This guy doesn't have any luck though, and there's a tappin' on the window with a voice reminding him that 'You can look but you better not touch boy/Mess around and you'll end up in dutch, boy'. Though the song is lighthearted, it manages to indict an entire system of relationships.

The next two songs are slower, more melancholy ballads, and in one sense both about being in dutch. *I Wanna Marry You* is probably the song on this album that inspired more female fantasies than any other, where in the softest tones Bruce offers himself as possible salvation to a woman 'raising two kids alone in this mixed up world' adding that it must be a 'lonely life for a working girl'. In a real world there are a lot of women in this situation (maybe it's her husband singing *Hungry Heart*) and the best you can hope is that he doesn't love her out of pity because she never smiles and never speaks, begging the question of what is her appeal. Part of the singer's motivation comes from recalling his father's words before he died, 'that true, true love was just a lie'. He then went to his grave with a broken heart, and though the singer would like to avoid that same fate, there's a sense that while their love may be beautiful, it's too selfless to believe.

The title song deals with another kind of marriage, a semi-forced one, and it's a difficult song to write about. It's linked to so many of Bruce's songs, as well as traditions and songs by other artists. Flannery O'Connor, one of Bruce's favorite authors, has a story called *The River* and, while Woody Guthrie's music was influencing Bruce at the time, the clearest reference here is to Hank William's classic *Long Gone Lonesome Blues*. There is also a whole tradition of 'river' songs ranging from *Good Night Irene* ('Sometimes I get a great notion, to jump in the river and drown') to *Take Me To The River*. On top of it all the couple are familiar characters, and the song is almost literally a continuation of the saga of the singer and Mary from *Thunder Road* where, as one fan put it, they ran off together, he got her in trouble and *The River* is their next chapter.

The arrangement is sparse and moody with piano, harmonica and Bruce's voice dominating. With masterful strokes Bruce sketches whole worlds in a few lines, starting with the singer who comes 'from down in the valley/Where minister, when you're young/They bring you up to do like your Daddy done'. This refers again to the binding ties of tradition, but one irony here is that the reality of his characters is one that Bruce himself has thus far rejected — marriage. He'd spoken earlier about how there was no room in his life for a woman, besides, 'I don't want to write no married music'. What he's written here is material that few married people could approach because it hits too close to home. The story line really begins with 'Then I got Mary pregnant/And, man that was all she wrote'. He then goes on to write quite a story, and although it's one that everybody knows, few people have been so precise in describing a shotgun wedding as going 'down to the courthouse/And the judge put it all to rest'. Needless to say the wedding doesn't really put anything to rest, and after making the crucial connections between their problems and the fact that 'lately there ain't been much work on account of the economy' the repercussion is that 'all the stuff that seemed so important just vanished right into the air'. There is a hint that they may be able to surmount their considerable obstacles by recalling the purity of their early love 'but those memories come back to haunt me, they haunt me like a curse'. This is a typical reaction to the past throughout all Bruce's songs, where a happy memory can become a curse because of the question it provokes; 'is a dream a lie if it don't come true/Or is it something worse'. The answer is inferred and in an example of Springsteen's writing at its best, the question leads to the next action where he asks 'Is it something worse/that sends me/Down to the River/though I know the river is dry'. The river is a symbol of life and rebirth and you are left asking whether the river is permanently dry, if hope and love are really dead.

*Point Blank* is the coldest song on *The River*, the story of a woman who 'grew up where young girls grow up fast'. What she doesn't realize is that while she took what she was handed and left behind what was asked, 'what they asked baby wasn't right'. The singer is always the hero, and that's okay when he can drop lines like 'tomorrow's fall in number/in number one by one/You wake up and you're dying/you don't even know what from'. The message, though grimmer than usual, is familiar; 'Point blank, did you forget how to love, girl did you forget how to fight/Point blank they must have shot you in the head/

Springsteen and Seger at Ann Arbor, Michigan, October 1980

Cause point blank/Bang bang baby you're dead'. The lifestyle is similar to *Sherry Darling* with its welfare checks and poverty but this woman's fate is sealed — she's given up. To his credit, Bruce manages to bring her story to life before writing her off.

The next song is about a lively dead man, whom Springsteen has called 'an anachronism', and he's called the song a gas guzzler. It's a song about a world that's on its way out and he takes his character and his audience on one last joy ride before it's all over. He also uses a photo of *Cadillac Ranch* on the lyric sheet, and brings alive the images in the song, where the Caddies look like half-buried dinosaurs. Bruce summons the ghosts of some famous cars and drivers (James Dean in that Mercury '49...even Burt Reynolds in that black Trans Am) and says they're all gonna meet at the — he even leaves funeral instructions in the song: 'Well buddy when I die throw my body in the back/And drive me to the junkyard in my Cadillac'. But after a ride in that little bit of heaven on earth he decides he's not ready to go yet, telling the little girlie that 'You're my last love baby you're my last chance/Don't let 'em take me to the Cadillac Ranch!' That Cadillac, 'long and dark shiny and black' suddenly becomes a hearse in the last line and it 'took my little girl away'.

*I'm A Rocker* is a crazy anthem full of boasting and superhero references emphasizing that he's a rocker and when a rocker's in love it means going all the way, every day and beats all else. There's some irony in having *Fade Away* follow this number since, just as in the Buddy Holly original, it's really about *not* fading away. In this song a situation develops where another man becomes a real threat (as opposed to *I'm A Rocker*, where the rival is described as 'some jerk who was tall, dark and handsome') because the woman says she's 'found another man who does things' to her that he can't. She tells him that no matter what he does that it's all over, but he can't accept it imploring that 'I don't wanna fade away'. While every connection can't be pointed out, the overall sense of this album is that the stories and characters are somewhat interchangeable and interrelated, so that the fate of the woman could be that of the subject in *Point Blank*, or the course of events could roll them right into *Stolen Car*.

The couple who part company in *Fade Away* 'got married and swore we'd never part/Then little by little we drifted from each other's heart'. The main character in *Stolen Car* sings that 'At first I thought it was just restlessness/That would fade as time went by and our love grew strong', but instead the river dries up and 'In the end it was something more I guess that tore us apart and made us weep'. He then takes to driving a stolen car — a symbol of his desperation — hoping to get caught since if he doesn't, he travels in the fear that 'in this darkness I will disappear'. The link to *Fade Away* is strong and the last line echoes a song as far back as *Night*. The disappointment and disillusionment that plagues so many of these characters is brought home by a line given to the wife; 'she said last night she read those letters (from when their love was 'young and bold') and they made her feel one hundred years old'. Keep in mind that *no one* in rock music is a hundred years old.

FINALLY. LON...
BRUCE
AND THE E

ON IS READY
RINGSTEEN
STREET BAND
FOR
DEON

Bruce waits in the wings for an encore at Wembley, June 1981

With the last side there's one more all out rock tune to start things off, but the story of *Ramrod* is just a reprise and with everything that's gone before it, the listener knows more than the characters who think they're gonna tear outta town, maybe go to a cute little chapel nestled in the pines, across the county line, and then go ramroddin' 'forevermore'. It's like a flashback, a high-idle dream and match for *Cadillac Ranch*.

By the time the last few songs come around the references are coming so thick and fast that they're difficult to untangle. Dave Marsh made the point that the end of the album works like blinds being pulled down one by one but although it's summation, the songs also point to the future, which in Bruce's case means the next album.

*The Price You Pay* is a line that appears in several songs, and it is one of Springsteen's main preoccupations. On one level the concept of prices and paying is integral to American life, rather in contrast to freedom, which is the dream. The theme is also as big as life itself and, since everything has its repercussions, one choice might exclude several others, a situation over which Springsteen has expressed frustration. Like the ties that bind, the price you pay is seen as something inescapable but the emphasis here is on choice ('You choose the chance you take') and on making peace with your choices, or as Bruce puts it, 'You learn to sleep at night with the price you pay'. After the first chorus the song takes a major turn and the people in the song get caught up in 'a dream where everything goes wrong' and the fight commences as in *Badlands* and *Promised Land*. Here again Bruce is addressing a woman, and like the one in *I Wanna Marry You*, she's 'a little girl down on the strand/With that pretty little baby in your hands'. He encourages her to run even though all the others that have run forward get to 'where the dark of night holds back the light of the day', where they have to stand and fight for the price they've paid. The singer tells her that 'just across the county line, a stranger passing through put up a sign' and it counts the men fallen away to the prices they've paid. In the final lines the singer swears to her that 'before the end of the day/I'm gonna tear it down and throw it away'. The stranger here is the vague 'they' that began to creep into earlier songs, and this is a battle cry not only against 'them' and against the price being too high but the fact that there is any price tag at all! There is also a reference to the story of Moses and here Bruce says that he 'could not enter the chosen land/On the banks of the river stayed/To face the price you pay'. Not only does Bruce claim himself bearer of the Eleventh Commandment ('Let It Rock') but, like Moses, his own mission is also to lead people out of slavery. But he doesn't want to be a martyr either, nor the artist-as-martyr that is one idea behind Hank Williams' *Long Gone Lonesome Blues* in which Bruce found both title and inspiration. Hank sang 'I'm gonna find me a river/And Lord, I'm gonna pay the price/I'm goin' down in it three times/But Lord I'm only comin' up twice'. Bruce sees other ways to pay the price.

*Drive All Night* is a perfect link between the past and the future, another love song where the woman is gone, hinting at Bruce's testament to that subject on *Born In The U.S.A.*

Here he still wants to drive all night, for her and with her, away from the fallen angels, calling strangers and the fire on the edge of town. Here, as on other songs, the concept of the couple is viewed as a safe haven. With the focus on the strength of the man and woman together, Bruce sings lines which sound like the Post Office creed set to music, but he puts so much emotion into 'through the wind, through the rain, the snow...' that the clichés, as is often the case under his influence, come to life. Not only does this refer back to *Darkness* and songs like *Prove It All Night*, but its language and sentiments also lay the groundwork for *Cover Me* and *Dancing In The Dark*.

Drawing again on the country music genre, Bruce borrowed a title from Roy Acuff for *Wreck On The Highway*. It's also an image that he's used before, but this song doesn't have the high drama of *Lost In The Flood*. It's simple and understated with a country style arrangement that is typical of many of the ballads on *The River*. The story concerns a man who foresees his own possible fate in a wreck on a dark road where he is the only witness. The dying man speaks only one line, the 'Mister won't you help me please' that would characterize the relationships on *Nebraska*. Finally the ambulance comes and takes him away (to Riverside) but the image haunts the singer and the final verse runs; 'Sometimes I sit up in the darkness/And I watch my baby as she sleeps/Then I climb in bed and I hold her tight/I just lay there awake in the middle of the night/Thinking about the wreck on the highway'. This song is an appropriate end to the album since the main character actually has a woman by his side, and though the effect of the wreck is to drive home an appreciation, it also brings with it a hint of fear and the cloud of death. True to the rest of his work, this final song has an ambiguous feeling of contradictory possibilities left open and, while some things are put to rest, for every dilemma that's resolved, a new one is presented.

What was clear at the time of release in 1980 was that the record was masterful. In fact, the only real problems arose when some master tapes were stolen for bootlegging purposes, though the theft was quickly discovered and security was tightened. Bruce also teamed up with CBS in an attempt to sue various bootleggers in another effort to regain artistic control. Although the fans' demands for his material was insatiable, Springsteen more than most artists is conscious of delivering a work of art and he is far more scrupulous than any bootlegger could be. (Have you seen any pictures like the one on the back of *The River* on a bootleg album?)

One of Bruce's professed aims with this double LP was to balance the exuberance of *Born To Run* with the more tragic and isolated vision of *Darkness*. That approach could also describe *Born In The U.S.A.*, though it also accounts for the seemingly contradictory approaches and feelings of the songs on *The River*. Commenting on his approach to the subject matter, he recalled: 'I just said, I don't understand all these things. I don't see where all these things fit. I don't see how all these things can work together! It was because I was always focusing on some small thing; when I stepped back, they just made a sense of their own. It

was just a situation of living with all these contradictions. And that's what happens. There's never any resolution. You have moments of clarity, things become clearer to you that you didn't understand before. But there's never any making ends meet or finding any type of long-standing peace of mind about something.' The fact that Bruce accepts contradictions but still tries to resolve them (a couple at a time and theme by theme, and without trying to impose any ironclad rules) is one of the things that makes him such an outstanding songwriter and artist. The other thing that makes him an exception is that he sees as well as presents things in human terms, rather than merely imposing an idea or a system upon the characters.

He also sees his audience as composed of real human beings and in increasingly international terms. Following *The River* there was a triumphal world tour, and even as he was recording Bruce had his audience in mind, saying 'That's what I thought about in the studio. I thought about

going out and meeting people I don't know. Going to France and Germany and Japan and meeting Japanese people and French people and German people, meeting them and seeing what they think, and being able to go over there with something. To go over there with a pocketful of ideas or to go over there with just something, to be able to take something over. And boom! To do it!'

He did go and he took a lot with him. Aside from performance, which is in the universal language of theatre, he took songs that were in English and set in America, but the European fans were able to appreciate what the Americans sometimes miss — the universal quality of his themes and the human truth in his treatment of them. Due to a combination of all these factors, *The River* and the follow-up tour established Bruce in the same terms that the Germans use to describe his music. He was a 'monsterhit' and for all the right reasons. He was singing and playing like no one else, saying the things people *needed* to hear.

# EIGHT
# THE PRICE YOU PAY

**As an indication of how far Bruce had come, there were very few negative reviews of The River World Tour. What complaints there were came from those critics who were happy enough to pick over the old dry bones, but who had no real feeling for what he was doing. The fans were with him and that's what really counted.**

Bruce surprised most people with his next release, challenging almost everyone's assumptions about him. *Nebraska* fulfilled John Hammond's prophecy that Bruce would someday make an album in a 'pure' folk style, although it came about less through calculation (he is after all 'not a planning type guy') than artistic necessity. Springsteen himself seems to have been somewhat surprised by the kind of songs he was writing. The album has a mysterious quality, a sort of inscrutability: Bruce managed to really let go of himself at the writing stage, and yet maintain control over the final form. He had once likened his record company's demand for a hit single to asking Michelangelo to paint a picture of his parents before being allowed to do the Sistine Chapel. To cannibalize the analogy, *Nebraska* is the musical equivalent of some of Michelangelo's later work, which has all the conceits of art but with a rawness of feeling and directness of expression that makes it seem artless.

This might seem a rather partisan introduction to an album which many have found easier to write off than write about. However, this album could easily outlast everything in Springsteen's catalogue. Its place in music history is somewhere beside the hotel room tapes of Robert Johnson and the recordings of Hank Williams. Not only do his songs share the same raw intensity as the blues numbers which inspire them, but *Nebraska* sees Springsteen turn to that under-used yet timeless form, the ballad. The songs' subjects come straight out of the best country music, as do the arrangements, the most immediately striking facet of the album. The stark four-track production, using just voice, guitar and harmonica, make all the multi-track productions of the last fifteen years look like soul-less aberations. While many see this album as a purely retrograde step, in fact Springsteen has cleared out a lot of

debris while raising the larger questions of what actually constitutes progression.

To many people the most fascinating aspect of the album was the production. After all, there is no E Street Band, not even a drum unless the guitar is considered as a percussion instrument. But beyond this is a new depth to these songs, more ambivalent and contradictory than anything that had preceeded it. On one level the characters, like the cover photo, are typified by their constricted vision. They see the world in stark terms, like the murderer of the title track explaining his action with: 'Well, sir I guess there's just a meanness in this world'. By the same token these concerns are universal and the vision of one character is usually balanced (and sometimes reinforced) by the song that follows.

As for the actual production of the album, what you hear is basically a songwriter's demo tape, though with so much poured into it by the singer-player, and with a spare sound so appropriate for the songs, that when the band tried to perform them they lost more than they gained by second takes and extra instruments. So upon the advice of his product manager at CBS, Bruce took the tapes (which the cover says were 'recorded in new Jersey by Mike Batlin on a Teac Tascam Series 144 4-track cassette recorder') and they were carefully mastered to produce the sound you hear. And whether or not he fully intended it, he made a significant statement in giving this 4-track version of his music to the public, because at a time when a lot of young musicians (and fans) were having their heads turned by high technology and bogus industry wisdom, he stripped the music down and exposed *that* as the crucial element. He did the same thing with the one video that he released in conjunction with *Nebraska*.

What you hear then, is what one fan considered the special beauty of the album; Bruce Springsteen playing all by himself, in his (or your) living room. The sense of intimacy is heightened by his habit of addressing the listener in his songs. Bruce had done this before, but about half the songs on *Nebraska* have a 'mister'; an anonymous listener or sometimes literally a judge or this state trooper, deejay, etc. So the listener is called upon to judge...and that

Gary U.S. Bonds guests with Springsteen and the E. Street Band

involvement is a crucial aspect of the stories and the storytelling.

The tale and its telling in the opening song, *Nebraska*, set the mood for the entire album. It's the story of Charlie Starkweather also the subject of the film *Badlands*, and Springsteen succeeds remarkably in getting into the head of the mass murderer — a type recognized world-wide as a uniquely American phenomenon. The blank and colloquial expression along with the unexpected thoughts and sentiments (when he goes to the electric chair he wants his 'pretty baby sittin' right here on my lap') make the story come alive. It describes a world where there's just a hairline distinction between taking and killing, and while the rest of the album backs off slightly from this precipice, most of the others have nothing left but the 'debts no honest man can pay'. The vision is generally bleak, but by the end a few notes of hope and touches of humanity manage to struggle through the meanness of this album's world.

*Atlantic City* makes for a geographical change, and it also has a source in a film, this time Louis Malle's eponymous movie, though it's also a place that Springsteen knows well. The song is about the mob, some changes and another small-time hustler and his girlfriend. The song begins with the line, they 'blew up the chicken man...now they blew up his house too' which gives a hint to what the *Mansion On The Hill* and all the other houses signify. They're concrete symbols of the lives that inhabit them, and in this song the house has to be obliterated along with its owner. The story line echoes Malle's film, but Springsteen introduces his own interpretation, adds a 'maybe' which throws the questions raised back in the listeners' lap. Talking about the corruption and rackets as well as their luck which 'may have died' and 'our love which may be cold', the chorus muses on the possibility that 'maybe everything that dies someday comes back'. It's something to be pondered in terms of whether or not it's true, and if so, what the differences would be. The song also recalls *Meeting Across The River* since the only way to get out of a financial and psychic bind is to do 'a little favor' for 'this guy'. The endless treadmill of debt is given a universal dimension via the name of the bank, the Central Trust, where all the characters have placed their savings. He chooses to take out what's left and buy 'two tickets on that coast city bus'.

This song also recalls a common criticism of Springsteen's work; that all his characters are 'losers'. The man in this song is afraid to get caught on the wrong side of that winners and losers line and so turns to crime, but these characters and their situations reflect the valid view that, given the odds against most people achieving anything, (whether their dream is real or illusory) the only option is to go outside the law. The only problem with the criminal option is that the outlaws basically want the same things as the people in the mansions (as Bruce put it 'poor man wanna be rich, rich man wanna be king. A king ain't happy till he rules everything') but they just don't have the law and police on their side. They're still striving for that mansion; the story changes if they get there.

*Mansion On The Hill* is understated in its drama; it's moody and blue and conjures images ranging from the film *Days Of Heaven* to the Hank Williams song *The Mansion On The Hill*. The Williams song is the most significant source, because even though Hank was looking at the loveless mansion with a woman in it who wouldn't return his affection, the dichotomy here is the same. In Springsteen's song the fortress on the hill has no human face, just a symbolic position above the mill town and the people living their lives below. There's no recrimination, Bruce just paints the picture for you. It could be symbolic of America but he doesn't write one-dimensional songs, and an introduction to this one in performance also refers to its personal significance. He talks about how his father used to drive him out to a big white house like the one in the song, and how it has now become a symbol in his own dream landscape. As he described it: 'It became very mystical, like a touchstone. And now when I dream, I'm sometimes outside the gate looking in...and sometimes I'm the man inside'. The people in the song are outside, looking up, and though some have criticized Bruce for not writing from the point of view of 'the man inside', that too is incorporated in his vision. The point he forgot to make is that the same gate that keeps him outside in one dream, is what keeps him inside in the next.

From the mill town it's on to Mahwah and the auto plant that closed and created another casualty in the process. (By the way, the newspapers should be up there with books, records, and films as sources of inspiration.) This guy's name is Ralph, but after he got drunk, killed a man and got sentenced, he's forever known as *Johnny 99*. Although this song was covered by Johnny Cash (as was *Highway Patrolman*), it is one of the album's more rocking tunes, belying some of the heavier lines. This song refers to a brand of justice so callous that the judge is gonna let the sentence fit the crime 'Prison for 98 and a year and we'll call it even/Johnny 99'. Johnny's allowed to speak his piece to the judge, but by then he's already made his own peace and figures 'well your honor I do believe that I'd be better off dead/And if you can take a man's life for the thought that's in his head' he recommends that they put him right on the execution line. One of the things that makes *Nebraska* so incredible is the type of speech Bruce gives to his characters, which is not only characterized by flat delivery, but by the gritty honesty of people who are beyond judgment. After Johnny talks about the 'debts no honest man can pay' and the fact that they were taking his house away, his comment is 'Now I ain't sayin' that makes me an innocent man' because 'it was more'n all this that put this gun in my hand'. If you've listened to his last few albums you can probably figure out what the 'more'n all this' is.

The depth of this album becomes most apparent on *Highway Patrolman*, where a character who would previously have been a faceless 'Maximum Lawman' starts off by telling his name, then a story which wraps up a whole lifestyle and chunk of history while debunking one kind of law for another. The Patrolman has a brother who 'ain't no good' (Frankie was in Vietnam, but it's been the same 'come down' ever since they were kids). The song

chronicles their relationship, but the details are more than just coloring and they open the song into an epic vision. The song is about blood ('nothin' feels better than blood on blood'), loyalty, and its primacy in a time when nothing else can be counted on. The patrolman lets his brother escape a murder, and his explanation is as point blank as anyone's: 'Well, if it was any other man, I'd put him straight away/But when it's your brother sometimes you look the other way'. It's a case of injustice, right? But the point is that there isn't any real 'legal' justice, (as in *Johnny 99*) more primary codes and ties will supercede the imposed law. So the law here is brotherly love and at their best they even share Joe's wife (they're 'takin' turns dancing with Maria as the band played *Night Of The Johnstown Flood*). The reference to the flood hints at the tragic overtones of the song, though that was a natural disaster,

and this one's largely social. The picture he paints of the brothers is fleshed out with references to social, political and economic history, though the emphasis as always is on how these things relate to and effect his characters. Bruce's writing had become so concentrated and his sense of characterization so accurate, that it would take another chapter to analyze all that he conjures in 5 lines; 'Well,

Franky went in the army back in 1965/I got a farm deferment/Settled down took Maria for my wife/But them wheat prices kept on droppin' till it was like we were gettin' robbed/Franky came home in '68 and me I took this job'.

*State Trooper* shows the other side of the coin to *Highway Patrolman*. The singer here is one of the 'other men' that the patrolman would normally put straight away.

He's driving in a nightmare version of Chuck Berry's New Jersey Turnpike (from *You Can't Catch Me*) and all you know is that he's got nothing — including license or registration — but that he's 'got a clear conscience 'bout the things that I done'. You never find out what he did (is he driving a *Stolen Car*?) but what's disturbing here is the potential for what he might do. You have the sense that he's asking the trooper not to stop him because one of them will have to die. And going back to what all the characters since *The River* have had in common (and he doesn't) he muses about the trooper 'Maybe you got a kid maybe you got a pretty wife, the only thing I got's been botherin' me my whole life'. You know what he's passing through — refinery's glow, where black rivers flow and the radio's jammed with all talk stations — and though all the reasons for his desperation aren't clear, the fact of it is. He sings that he's on his last prayer and wants somebody (The Lone Ranger?) to hear it as he cries 'Hi ho silver-o deliver me from nowhere'. This is the landscape conjured on *Born To Run* grown totally desperate, and though it's hard to tell how much of the LP's sound quality was there in the original recording, the reverb on the 'whoops' helps to convey what words can only sketch. And the final cry of 'deliver me' is heard again and becomes another theme on *Nebraska*.

*Used Cars* is a song for fans of Bruce the man, because it's clearly got autobiographical elements, but to see it solely in those terms is to miss much of its meaning. The idea of a 'brand new used car' points to the discrepancy between people's aspirations and what they actually get. His ('the') parents might be resigned to this, but the singer isn't gonna be satisfied as easily. When they drive the car home, 'the neighbors come from near and far...I wish he'd just hit the gas and let out a cry and tell 'em they can kiss our asses goodbye'. This is another of the songs partly inspired by recollections of childhood, but the story is told by one who's grown bitter. The theme of who sides with who, and why, is driven home with the salesman 'tellin' us all 'bout the break he'd give us if he could but he just can't'. No one has the power to break out; all that makes the son (the singer) different is his dreams. He sings 'Now mister the day the lottery I win (or when 'my number comes in')/I ain't gonna ride in no used car again'. It's a hope all right, but he's just another one dreamin' while he's goin' down.

While *Nebraska* began with an image like that which opens *Thunder Road*, *Open All Night* starts off with the same sort of car customizing description which begins in *Racing In The Street*. The setting is again the Turnpike and the song runs parallel to *State Trooper*, although this character's desperation is of a slightly different quality. Driving through 'early north Jersey industrial skyline' he's on his way home and thinkin' 'bout his baby'. Problem is that 'the boss didn't dig me he put me on the nightshift/It's an all night run to get back to where my baby lives.' The memory of his first meeting with his girl, Wanda, cheers him up for a while, but the present really isn't so great. Like the driver in *State Trooper* he's gotta worry about gettin' stopped and all the while he's driving in the 'wee wee hours where your eyes get itchy and your mind gets hazy' with

three more hours to go while the radio's jammed upon with gospel stations 'lost souls callin' long distance salvation' What makes these two songs different from pieces like *Night* where the song ends by driving on into the night, is the focus on the reality of a late night drive, and more importantly on the state of mind that the night drive exacerbates, leaving him literally crying into a void. He calls out to the nearest voice 'Hey Mr deejay woncha hear my last prayer/hey ho rock 'n' roll deliver me from nowhere'. He's afraid that he will really disappear into that darkness. Music and voice provide two much needed links to humanity. It's Bruce's contribution.

The imagery of the next song, *My Father's House*, is echoed in *Downbound Train*, with obvious links to *Adam Raised A Cain*, *Independence Day* and *Used Cars*. The song is both about a dream and about seeking a dream in the real world. It conveys the fact that while the past is gone, some images and memories remain as living beacons. But the song ends with the fact of death, and the realization that it's now too late to settle accounts, 'our sins lie unatoned'. Dream songs have recently become a feature of Springsteen's repertoire and so far they're fairly similar. The dreamscape always includes a structure (a house) which is both the real and symbolic touchstone for certain associations. But the dreamer wakes to find that the real structure is empty and the reconciliation becomes one with the self and the past rather than the subject of the dream.

The album's final song, *Reason To Believe*, is sung in an appropriately amazed tone, since the stories it tells in each verse are about something dead or gone (a dead dog that's still being poked, a wayward man etc.), but still 'at the end of every hard earned day, people find some reason to believe'. Considering the religious imagery in this song — which includes a description of a baptism, funeral and marriage — it shouldn't be too surprising that one of the most inciteful reviews was in a magazine called Christian Century. The writer asks the question that the song provokes: 'Do they find that reason because they need to or because hope and purpose are real? Springsteen does not or cannot say.' Bruce did say later that '*Nebraska* was about a breakdown in values, a spiritual crisis' and the fact that he leaves the listener with a glimmer of hope (even if it's as rationally unjustifiable as the 'meanness in this world') is significant and true to form. As Mr. McFadden put it, 'Like all effective imagery, that with which Springsteen closes is ambiguous, inviting interpretation through personal experience. The image, like the album, is disturbing, haunting and somehow hopeful. In its many layers and complex textures, *Nebraska* is a major work of art.

If a lot of fans were disappointed in the surface bleakness and lack of dance beat, it was just a matter of time before these thematic and stylistic explorations would pay off in an exuberance earned by Bruce's confrontation with the shadows lurking behind Truth, Justice, and The American Way. His next attempt was to produce what he called 'survival music', which was just what his own characters were begging for as they drove uttering that last prayer of 'Hey ho rock 'n' roll, deliver me from nowhere!'

# NINE

# I'M A ROCKER

Springsteen may have reached a new audience with *Nebraska*, but his hardcore support is, and always has been, a fairly traditional group of fans. Most will almost automatically buy anything he puts out, but the fact was that soon after *Nebraska* was released, people started looking for a follow-up to *The River*! What he gave them was better than that, because while it fulfilled the needs of the rockers with a vengeance, *Born In The U.S.A.* also incorporated ballads similar in both form and content to those in both *The River* and *Nebraska*. Robert Christgau commented that the 'sound and vision' which Springsteen and Jon Landau pursued 'evolve so slowly they appear to progressives not to change at all'. But in fact Springsteen's music has evolved enormously, so that it's also true that the records which gained him national recognition now seem relatively murky and overblown even to those who didn't mind those flaws at the time. In that sense *Born In The U.S.A.* represents a leap, but in a direction that has been quite consistent. And aside from mentioning the singing and songwriting that alone make the record an enormous feat, Christgau speaks of Springsteen bringing rock 'n' roll's traditional, 'affirm-in-the-negative' approach to a new pitch of consciousness. And not surprisingly the question of what Springsteen is affirming, and indeed why, have become the major issues of this LP.

Artists are always responding to their times in one way or another, and the fact that Springsteen should bring out an album called *Born In The U.S.A.* emblazoned with a picture of his ass and the stripes of the American flag in the summer of 1984 is surely significant. A good many people see war looming on the horizon, and 'the war' makes it into a couple of Springsteen's songs. Where one stands has become less and less a theoretical issue and Springsteen has chosen to place himself right in the thick of election year arguments about nationalism, patriotism, etc. In fact, he is rather better at raising issues than answering them, even though there is a definite sense that these things will be forced to some kind of resolution. While he will undoubtedly let his music speak for him, others are increasingly trying to make it speak for them. In the wake of the Los Angeles Olympics accompanying an orgy of jingoistic flag-waving, WNEW DJs urged their listeners to wear red, white and blue to Springsteen concerts because it would 'look good'. One critic commented that Springsteen had 'earned the right' to use the American flag, but he certainly didn't earn that right by being anyone's puppet. He's done it by speaking to and for the people, however confused and contradictory they (and he) may be.

*Born In The U.S.A.* also came out with great expectations and a major publicity campaign. One of the most intriguing rumors surrounding the release was the fact that the album was originally to have had the working title of *Murder Inc.* (Some have postulated that he will use that title and some of the sixty odd songs recorded during those sessions as the basis for his next LP, and though the title is suggestive and the songs are likely excellent, his orientation will probably change in time for his next release.) Most other pre-release rumors revolved around Steve Van Zandt and his relationship — or lack of one — to Springsteen. The members of the E Street Band all assume, and are given, a lot of freedom by the The Boss, but Miami stands out, both because of his independent output — two solo LPs and a film — and because he is more prone to making public comments than anyone, including Bruce. Furthermore, Little Steven's output has been pointedly political, leading to accusations of having prostituted his art in favor of politics. He considers the two to be integral; but many see his political outlook as contradictory, causing him to be dubbed a political cartoonist and so on. Of course Springsteen's music has been interpreted politically; but the difference is that his politics are rarely explicit, rising rather from the subject matter of his songs. Little Steven on the other hand has taken to wearing his rather muddled concerns on his sleeve.

The friendship between the two goes way back, and is the subject of a note by each man on the liners of their most recent albums. Van Zandt thanks Springsteen for the long friendship, help and inspiration, and Springsteen bids Van Zandt goodbye and good journey in Italian. The reasons for parting are not clear, but there were rumors that at one point during the recording process Springsteen became so

After three and a half hours on stage Bruce is starting to flag

enraged about something that he tore into the studio and erased all of Van Zandt's guitar parts. In fact Van Zandt's contribution to *Born In The U.S.A.* is major and, contrary to a time-honored tradition (since *Darkness*) of listing the players in alphabetical order, Springsteen gives Van Zandt billing over himself in the credits. All of this implies a lack of animosity between the two and it seems that their main differences are matters of perspective and therefore direction. Something of the character of this can be seen in Van Zandt's comment to Rolling Stone that he couldn't be concerned about the album's release date 'cause there's forty-two wars going on in the world right now'. This is a fact which Springsteen is no doubt also aware of, but rather than writing a song for each one, he more subtly explores the basis for all of them.

In fact, the opening title song sets the context (and time frame) of the album with reference to the Vietnam War, which from then on becomes any war past or future. Rock 'n' roll jumps right out of the first grooves with Max Weinberg's drumming paving the way for a lively, stripped down and 'fresh' approach to the music. *Born In The U.S.A.* is at least one song where the first take stood, and as Roy Bittan explained it, he just played it, Bruce sang his part and it didn't get any better. As usual the whole band's performance is superlative, though Weinberg and Bittan should get a good share of the glory for the sound and feeling that characterizes *Born In The U.S.A.* They're the first ones you hear, though following upon the power drumming and fugue-like synthesizer a gnarled sounding voice enters to tell his story. Putting things more bluntly than ever, this Vietnam Vet says that he was born in a 'dead man's town' ('first kick he took was when he hit the ground'). Bruce only has to sketch in the background like in the line where he explains why he went to a foreign land 'to go and kill the yellow man'; it's 'cause he got 'in a little hometown jam', which is par for the course for most of Bruce's male characters. On this album certain realities are driven home more than ever, as most of the characters on the first side of the LP have been in some kind of jam or another that has either landed them in prison or in a job that's indistinguishable from a life sentence. Springsteen's vision of the U.S.A. is pretty grim; these aren't free people who 'end up like a dog that's been beat too much/Till you spend your whole life just coverin' up'. Bruce exposes some raw nerves here with lines like the one about his brother at Khe Sahn who was 'fighting off the Viet Cong' while 'they're still there and he's all gone'. Springsteen's sympathy for the character is clear, but the human toll is perceived in terms of society as a whole where mere survival has become paramount. He's been ten years 'burnin' down the road' and while he may be a 'cool rocking Daddy', he's also 'long gone' with 'Nowhere to run...nowhere to go'. The 'nowhere', from which those characters run, turns out to exist on all sides. As much as some of these characters want to retreat, that's not really possible either, though the possibility is explored in the next song.

*Cover Me* is the first of a few love songs on the album, and instead of looking for a lover who won't blow his cover, Bruce is looking for 'a lover who will come on in and cover me'. Much of this record is about people trying to shut out certain realities — and with good reason — though the overall effect isn't one of escapism. This song is about retreat, *serious* retreat, with its talk of 'bolt the door, don't let them find us', and with the plea to 'let our love blind us', but there is a reason which is stated clearly enough; 'This whole world is out there just trying to score/I've seen enough I don't want to see anymore'. The idea of creating an insular but satisfactory world with a lover has been explored before, but the world always manages to intrude somehow. As on the rest of the album, the lyrics alone can't convey the larger meaning which comes through in the style and spirit of its playing. Again Weinberg excelled himself, and it should be mentioned that he's recently come out with a book of interviews (called *The Big Beat*) featuring several of the great living rock drummers. He claims that what he learned from them had a direct effect on his drumming, and with this album he officially joins the ranks of the all time greats. This song also features the combined and sympathetic guitar work of Springsteen and Van Zandt which give a blues edge to an already edgy song.

*Darlington County* is the third song on the album and provides a break in the intensity that was building after only two numbers. This song is one of a few that can only be described as funny, which has less to do with the story than with the characters Bruce has created. He's given them lines that Lanford Wilson would be proud of, and he manages the vocal inflections to make them come alive. The male characters are so naive, that even the tragic ending (sort of) doesn't really register. In that sense it's related to earlier tunes like *Cadillac Ranch*, and though Springsteen might also describe the singer and his buddy Wayne as anachronisms, he's also celebrating the innocent spirit which is one of the things that Bruce seems to love most in rock music (and America?). As is the case with a couple of the other songs on the LP, *Darlington* makes rock 'n' roll — and what it stands for — a major element in the lives of the characters. The story is about two guys from New York City (really?) who are heading south; like the couple in *My Hometown* they migrate to follow the work, and they even have a 'union connection'. One irony here is that many factory jobs were moved south just because there were no unions down there. So they head down to *Darlington County* (a real place in South Carolina) and the line that explains the exuberant mood that prevails and accounts for all those 'Sha la las' in the chorus is that they 'drove eight hundred miles without seeing a cop/We got rock 'n' roll music blasting off the t-top!' Arriving in Darlington City in fine spirits, Bruce paints a really comical picture of these two 'big spenders' who tell girls things like 'today's your lucky day for sure all right'. These guys are the ultimate bumpkins — you can't imagine anyone taking them seriously with their talk of how their Daddy's each own one of the World Trade Centers and how 'for a kiss and a smile I'll give mine all to you'. The singer also invites the 'little girl' to 'take a seat on my fender' which happens to be the brand name of Bruce's guitar and it seems like an intentional inside joke, hinting

that there's always more to his songs than meets the eye. From the fender the action moves to the bumper, and when the singer decides to leave town after not seeing Wayne for seven days, he suddenly confronts 'the glory of the coming of the lord' i.e., 'Wayne handcuffed to the bumper of a state trooper's Ford'. From the make of the car to the *Battle Hymn Of The Republic*, the Sha la la chorus, and the number's opening on the Fourth of July you've got a song that could only have been written by Springsteen, and a strange one it is too. Mostly because it takes to an extreme a trend that's apparent on the whole album: that is, rock tunes that jump with joy while the lyrics work in direct contradiction.

*Working On The Highway* isn't literally a continuation of *Darlington*, but it's another version of the same story. Here the repeated chorus dominates the song, but again there is a solid narrative sketched into it. From a beginning that sounds like a description of just another dead-end job ('Workin' on the highway, all day long I don't stop') you slowly discover that thanks to his love for a little girl he goes out of bounds, steals her away from her parents and as a result gets put 'straight away'. Lyrically and thematically this one recalls *Nebraska* where the ever present prosecutor finds his way into the story. It also has that same blank language that implies no real guilt in the minds of the accused. Despite the heaviness of the lyrics this song has a bouncy beat that's reminiscent of the early rockers, and along with Danny Federici's tasteful organ tones and Bruce's innocent accepting voice, the full weight of what's going on doesn't hit you until the end of the song when he sings about how 'Me and the warden go swinging on the Charlotte County Road gang'. So this guy shares, with the others we've been introduced to, the same sense of captivity on varying lengths of rope. One word on Bruce's vocabulary: aside from 'glory' which finds its way into a few songs, the words 'union' and 'county' come up pretty frequently. While on the one hand the unions are labor unions, the important aspect for Bruce is the idea of unity and belonging that they conjure up. County, more often than not, isn't your own home territory so you're automatically suspect and more than likely to fall into the hands of the department of corrections.

*Downbound Train* is another return to the images and language of *Nebraska*. The singer tells his story to an anonymous 'mister' and again the themes are jobs, love, and loss in both. The tale moves in a downward spiral from losing a job in a lumber yard to work in a carwash where the worst thing that can happen does — 'all it ever does is rain'. Presumably tied in with his declining status, his girl tells him 'Joe, I gotta go, we had it once we ain't got it anymore', and that is really the beginning of the end. The song, like three of the four love songs on this album, is moody, dark and slow, in the vein of *The River* or *Nebraska*, and the ending is almost a direct reference and parallel to the central image and action in *My Father's House*. A dream of her calling for him prompts a return to their 'wedding house', but instead of finding her wanting him, the 'room was dark, our bed was empty'. These characters are all still feeling the pain or numbness of

recent losses or experiencing the realization of what was lost (and can't be regained) a long time ago.

The next track, *I'm On Fire*, continues the feeling of loss, pain and desperation. Its sparse arrangement features a rhythm ticking ominously away like a clock (or a heartbeat). For once the 'little girls' actually seem quite young and balance on the edge of danger. The flat speech of the male character verges on the insane, although what he desires is typical enough. At least this guy admits that he's got 'a bad desire', and while he claims that his desire can take her higher, he's just another one looking for some solace. Not unusual for Springsteen, but now the characters are in such pain that 'sometimes it's like, someone took a knife baby, edgy and dull, and cut a six inch valley through the middle of my soul'. He's in bad shape, with a freight train running through his head while he wakes with his sheets soaking wet, and though he's one of the farthest gone, he's also a kind of a composite of all the characters on the album's first side.

The second side of *Born In The U.S.A.* doesn't aim for quite the same sort of narrative unity, but includes a fair share of great songs, and while they comment on those included on the first side, these are generally more personal in origin and not so stridently fictional. The side opener of *No Surrender* has been dedicated to Little Steven in concert and performed as a solo acoustic number with a change in the final verse. The Van Zandt connection is obvious without the dedication; the song begins with the line 'We busted out of class had to get away from those fools/We learned more from a three minute record than we ever learned in school' and continues to describe those days when they swore blood brothers and made their vow ('Like soldier in the winter's night'); 'no retreat no surrender'. The structure of the song is interesting; like many here it begins in the past, goes farther backwards only to finally end in the present. As Bruce comes to the 'now' he says 'there's a war outside still raging/You say it ain't ours anymore to win' and while this seems to define Steven's attitude quite well, the singer wants 'to sleep beneath peaceful skies in my lover's bed' though he also knows what he's got are 'these romantic dreams in my head'. Besides changing the lyrics to state that he wanted to sleep 'in the twilight, beside the riverbed', he added a 'because' before the final chorus which managed to change his final position from escape to just a 'temporary' retreat. The implication is that the vow is still intact, begging the question of what is still worth fighting for. In classic rock fashion this tune features ensemble background vocals, including one 'La Bamba' (a former Juke) who could recently be seen playing at the Stone Pony though I don't have the latest schedule.

Taking a lighter turn, the boys swing into *Bobby Jean*, another song that strikes as personal because Bruce is singing about somebody hearing his song on the radio. While some have seen this song as another about Bruce and Little Steven, it also recalls the continuing saga of *Backstreets*. In this song some kind of reconciliation with the past is achieved. He regrets that Bobby Jean left without saying goodbye, and will miss the fact that there

Bruce and Ronnie Spector guest with Southside Johnny

'ain't nobody, nowhere nohow ever understand me the way you did', but he can admit the past is gone, so it's best to keep the memories and just say 'I miss you baby, good luck, goodbye'. The resentment and pain of the earlier songs has faded away but in some ways this is one of the saddest songs of all.

*Glory Days* could well have followed *Bobby Jean* but instead a song with the title *I'm Goin' Down* comes on. This song has *the* bounciest beat on the record, and the introduction of hand claps towards the end lifts it into ecstasy. Again the lyrics and music are *seemingly* out of sync, though here for a change we have a character who might just get out of his bind and go up instead of down. It's another story about a love grown cold, but this time it's become a little sadistic, rather than trying to raise each other up, 'lately girl you get your kicks from just driving me down'. While the verses are nice, it's the extended chorus with repeated 'downs' and 'knocka's' (which is 'knock' in rock lingo) that do the trick. Bruce really rediscovered the nonsense syllable for this LP, thus continuing the great rock tradition where 'Be Bop Alula' is considered by many the greatest lyric ever written. This is also a song that at some point might benefit by trading verses with a woman (since it could be his kisses that used to turn *her* inside out right?), and this becomes a distinct possibility for the first time now that Bruce has included a woman in his stage shows. Her name is Patty Scialfa and Bruce supposedly met her while she was singing in 'some bar'. (She was appearing with Cats On A Smooth Surface and had previously worked with Southside Johnny.) She's definitely got the rock 'n' roll spirit, and Bruce says he likes having her with them cause it 'gives a sense of community'. Her role in the early stages of the tour was fairly limited (she was on and off the stage all night) but there seems every reason to expand it.

*Glory Days* is another tune with that dancing-on-graves feel to it, and the singer is both inside and out, laughing at the others who content themselves with recollections of 'glory days' (could be personal or national). The people on this song are all drinking a little too much and end up laughing and then crying into their beer over what's passed by. The first verse is about a guy who was 'a big baseball player', the kind of guy Bruce might have envied at one point, but man, all he does now is talk about them 'glory days'. The same thing happens with a woman friend. She's alone with her kids like so many others, and when she feels like crying she thinks about them glory days too, 'glory days in the wink of a young girl's eye'. After seeing all this, the singer finds himself 'goin' to the well' and drinking his fill, and hoping that 'when I get old I won't sit around thinkin' about it but I probably will'. Getting back to Christgau's affirm-in-the-negative, this song is but another example, where if he says he probably will it means maybe there's a chance he won't, or at least that he won't cry too much. The woman in the second verse also recalls one of the singles Bruce released, a song called *Jersey Girl*. Tom Waites wrote it, but you'd never guess since the subject and treatment are so true to Bruce. There's one line about taking your 'brat' to your mothers so we can go out and have a good time, and it's a nice live version of the song if it happens to come your way.

*Dancing In The Dark* was the first single release from the album and has what amounts to the LP's most inspirational music, since on one level inspiration is the subject of the song. Starting with a guy who gets up in the evening but who 'ain't got nothing to say' you find out that he's also bored with himself and with his whole life. He echoes a statement made by David Byrne in *Seen And Not Seen* about wanting to change his clothes, his hair, his face, and considering that some people would like to see Bruce take a radical leap, it's interesting to hear one of his characters talk like that. Other things are familiar, like his plea that 'baby I could use just a little help', and though Bruce is talking about a 'love reaction' the song implies much more. The chorus line of 'You can't start a fire without a spark' echoes Mao's famous comment about how it only takes a single spark to start a prairie fire, but the metaphors are mixed (as in hired-gun equals studio musician or mercenary or...) and the meaning of all parts isn't equally clear. There are some great throwaway lines like 'They say you gotta stay hungry/Hey baby I'm just about starving tonight', or my favorite; 'I'm sick of sitting 'round here trying to write this book', but as usual the key lines are the final ones. Here Bruce is making a point about the repercussions of change, and they amount to a challenge as much as a warning. He sings, 'You can't start a fire without your little world falling apart/This gun's for hire...even if we're just dancing in the dark'. It seems like things could go farther and become clearer than just dancing in the dark, and this is a thread that some fans would like to see developed.

Typically, Springsteen throws in a good dose of ambiguity for the final song, returning to the theme of cyclic change, though the song's ending is open, leaving the resolution for the next album or for the listener. *My Hometown* is the most ballad-like and slowest song on the album, and it recalls *Independence Day* for a few reasons. There are the obvious references to his father and the passing of (and on) a tradition, as well as the almost verbatim lift from the other song when he sings about his hometown that it 'seems like there ain't nobody wants to come down here no more'. The jobs have gone 'and they ain't coming back' and though the singer and Kate talk about packing up their bags (and maybe heading south), you know that they'll probably end up in another dead man's town. This couple has the same feeling that there is little they can do, but they have to do *something*, even if it's only to decide to stay in their hometown. The singer here is thirty-five (Bruce's age as of this writing) and with a boy of his own, so he's thinking about the future (and about past and tradition) and this is where Springsteen leaves you at the end of this ride. There's a sense of imminent change, and though all these people are still alive by the end of the album their futures are by no means guaranteed.

Bruce has decided with this album to place himself in the hot seat, since his American identity (and fullbodied appreciation of things like cheeseburgers, Cadillacs and baseball) and his negative vision of the country look to be on a collision course. He might not want to draw the lines, but if they are drawn for him he will be forced to respond somehow. In the meantime he's leading, with an album that was Number One and with sold out concerts all over the world, and he's succeeded in doing what Mike Appel said should be done years ago. He's gotten America to look up and dance to the same three or four chords. Let's just hope everybody keeps dancing to the beat and not marching in time.

# TEN

# 'NO SURRENDER'

As soon as people heard a few chords from *Born In The U.S.A.* they were making comments like 'Now Bruce is up there with Elvis and the Beatles' — while others have thought so all along. Some have said that you can't even consider Bruce outside the world of rock'n'roll, and in a sense that's true. It's the world he *wants* to inhabit, and rock'n'roll is the artform that he's chosen. He realizes its limits and generally accepts them, because, although he might be considered a person of political or social consequence, he would rather be viewed as an artist, a musician, a performer, a person, and perhaps a person of cultural consequence.

He has accepted all of these mantles, though being seen as a guide, an inspiration, and generally Superhuman certainly takes a toll on him. He's intent on not letting his audience down, but when you consider all of the expectations — and how contradictory they are — you begin to get some idea of the difficulty of his position and yet how crucial his decisions are. At least to Bruce and his fans, and so for a moment I'd like to talk about Bruce Springsteen as a man and a rock'n'roller. Whatever influence he has is based on who Bruce Springsteen is and, as a consequence, what kind of music he makes. The context in which he does it is not simple and includes personal, artistic, business and social considerations. In order to cope with all of these things (let alone perform) Bruce has made a few significant changes in his life indicative of his desire to face all of these things while maintaining his reputation of excellence and integrity.

Part of his response to these pressures has been to adopt a diet and exercise regime which includes running and weightlifting. Evidently he's also got all the people who work for him doing the same thing because he's gotta have some help. In this regard, one quote comes to mind — Bruce mentioned to a Rolling Stone writer that 'when you're up against big business and politics, you gotta have some muscle'. Big business might be represented in his life by CBS Records and while Bruce, with the help of his fans, has more say than he used to with the company, new issues and new struggles are always forthcoming. One factor which almost all musicians have to contend with now is the pressure to make videos to accompany their work. Springsteen commissioned one for *Atlantic City* from the *Nebraska* album and it was anything but run of the mill. Done in a black and white documentary style, it stood out in both content and tone from everything which surrounded it, but fans (and probably CBS brass) still wanted to see his face. So Bruce consented to release a live tape of *Rosalita (Come Out Tonight)*, and that seemed to temporarily settle the issue. It offered a good glimpse of Bruce and the Band at work and at least satisfied the promotional needs of the record company. But as soon as *Born In The U.S.A.* was released, the demand resumed. At this point the pressure from all sides was increasing, since many people see Bruce as a potential silver screen idol (there has been no shortages of roles offered, or requests to use his music), and a person with an obvious filmic and storytelling sensibility. So why not just do a narrative video and star in it? Thus far he's balked, and while his reasons are no doubt justified, the result has been less than satisfying. He ended up having Brian De Palma film a 'live' version of *Dancing In The Dark*, and while it has its moments, the overall effect is self-conscious and thus embarrassing. Whatever the reasons behind this failure, it's clear that the pressure to make videos is not going to evaporate, so perhaps he will tackle the challenge head on next time.

Part of what seems to keep him from acting a part (even if he's playing himself) is that he's not particularly interested in capitalizing on his face, or prostituting himself for promotional purposes. After all, if he was seen on MTV nationally he might not be able to get away with things like his recent cross country road trip on which he was only recognized twice! There may however be an even more crucial issue which Bruce hinted at in a recent interview: 'Part of the thing is that when I write the song, I write it to be the movie — not to *make* a movie, to *be* a movie, like *Highway Patrolman* or *Racing In The Street*. It's only six minutes. You could really screw it up in an hour and a half'. You could also really screw it up in six minutes were it a typical music video, and since his media are words and music, he's right to be wary of a literal visual interpretation

(Left to right) Clarence Clemons, Bruce Springsteen, Gary W. Talent, Danny Federici, Nils Lofgren, Patti Scialfa

which would hammer down certain meanings whilst inadequately dealing with others. Bruce has said that, 'I look forward to getting into video, to see what can be done with it'. In the meantime he continues to focus on what he does best. (He had John Sayles direct a more appropriate video to *Born In The U.S.A..*)

During his recent World tour Bruce had people cheering for him every night and this has led to discussion on

bear) Springsteen may end up as the pioneer of rock'n'roll as circus; he's even introduced one song with the 'for children of all ages' rap and is quite conscious of his ringmaster role.

Another thing that the New York-New Jersey shows made clear is how truly fanatical and devoted Springsteen's fans are. Most people, if they went once, went twice, and the demand for tickets was unprecedented. This audience was *serious*. At any given moment half of the crowd (at least) was singing along, and whenever Bruce stopped there was a huge chorus there to fill in the gaps. And I'm not talking about the easy parts of the songs. Most people knew *all* the words to *all* the songs. It was a religious experience for most involved, which begs the question of how Bruce can reach out beyond the faithful and the already converted.

On the one hand, Springsteen doesn't seem to want to dilute his message or alienate the white middle and working class people that have always been his natural audience, but on the other there are elements that would have difficulty finding its way into one of his songs. This includes the world beyond the U.S.A. as well as certain styles of music that he has generally shied away from. He did have techno-wizard Arthur Baker (famous for his work with Afrika Bambaataa) do a *great* series of dance mixes for *Dancing In The Dark*, but so far he hasn't had a chance to go much further. Due to the racial/musical lines that still exist, his decision to continue playing a fairly pure brand of rock'n'roll might keep his music from being more broadly disseminated. The intention is not that Bruce should become more famous or richer, but that there is potentially something in his music for people who aren't even aware of its existence. Perhaps the breakthrough will come with *Born In The U.S.A.*

As for his commitment to rock'n'roll and how he sees his music, Bruce had these comments to make: 'Everything has its limitations and its ultimate possibilities, and you gotta test them to find out what they are. It's like those Italian westerns at the drive-in. I always loved it that they showed 'em all at once. That's the way I make these albums — so they get played all at once'. The unity of his work has already been emphasized and, while most fans do take the approach to his albums that Bruce describes, it might also be considered that something like *The Good, The Bad And The Ugly* stands pretty well on its own. So does *Born In The U.S.A.*, and though he's come so far already, there's no reason for him to stop now.

The main question is not really whether he'll continue to progress, but what direction it will take. The most frequent criticism of his work is also a wish that Springsteen would address his music more directly to different types and classes of people. Almost everyone feels the need for quality art to both represent them and speak to them, and this is exactly what Springsteen has provided over the years. But attempting to satisfy *all* the people is not only fraught with danger, it's well nigh impossible in the polarized nineteen-eighties. Depending on who and what Bruce Springsteen chooses to represent in his future output may mean the difference between solidifying his base,

everything from the evolution of his stage shows to the significance of his audience and his potential for further outreach. One thought that the shows prompted was that if Bruce doesn't want to do videos for a teen and adult audience, maybe he would consider doing something for children. This year he and Clarence were doing one of their lost-in-the-woods in New Jersey skits and it occurred to me that with his storytelling, acting and childlike innocence, kids might be a perfect audience. The introduction of Nils Lofgren in place of Little Steven also proved something that Bruce said a long time ago, that the band can change but he'll still continue. Lofgren added a lot to the shows, not the least of which is his ability to do flips while still hitting the right notes. With Nils by his side (and with the dancing

# REAGAN KNOWS WHO'S BOSS

## REAGAN KNOWS WHO'S BOSS

Who's the right wing's latest darling? Bruce Springsteen, to judge from the recent comments of President Reagan and conservative columnist George F. Will. "If all Americans . . . made their products with as much energy and confidence as Springsteen and his merry band," wrote Will in his September 13th column after attending a Springsteen show, "there would be no need for Congress to be thinking about protectionism." Will admitted he didn't have "a clue about Springsteen's politics."

Six days later, at a New Jersey rally, Reagan did Will one better. America's future, he said, "rests in the message of hope, in the songs of a man that so many young Americans admire, New Jersey's own Bruce Springsteen. Helping you make these dreams come true is what this job of mine is all about."

At press time, there was no comment from the Springsteen camp. And it remained unclear exactly which Springsteen songs Reagan's speech writers had been listening to. When one Reagan-campaign spokesman was informed that the president had referred to Springsteen, he replied: "Omigod. He didn't say 'this gun's for hire,' did he?"  —Christopher Connelly

possibly losing part of it, or expanding his audience to an unprecedented degree.

Some of the choices will belong to Bruce and some may be determined by larger social forces and trends. He could probably have predicted that *Born In The U.S.A.* would be embraced by people with a wide variety of interests and motivations, but it seems increasingly risky to allow that trend to continue much into the future. *My Hometown* was used to open a recent world series game, and though baseball lover Bruce may have approved of that choice, he had to draw the line when this tendency to capitalize on his assumed patriotism led to Ronald Reagan invoking his name for pointedly political ends. Reagan was unable to get Bruce on the podium with him, so instead decided to endorse Springsteen in an effort to ally himself with his message and his fans. Speaking in Hammontown, N.J., Reagan told his audience that 'America's future rests in a thousand dreams inside your hearts. It rests in the message of hope in songs of a man so many young Americans admire: New Jersey's own Bruce Springsteen. And helping you make those dreams come true is what this job of mine is all about.' In light of this and myriad other attempts to co-opt Springsteen's message, his 'job' is becoming more crucial and difficult. He will likely continue to let his music speak for him, as he did in response to Reagan's ploy. Said Bruce during one of his shows, 'The president was mentioning my name the other day and I kinda got to wondering what his favorite album musta been. I don't think it was the *Nebraska* album. I don't think he's been listening to this one...' at which point he launched into *Johnny 99*.

Bruce sings in *Dancing In The Dark* that 'this gun's for hire' and in *Johnny 99* that 'it was more 'n all this that put that gun in my hand'. It seems that Springsteen is ready for the fight and I look forward to seeing which targets he aims for. Chances are he'll hit them, and possibly make his best music ever in the process. That's my hope and I imagine it's yours as well.

# DISCOGRAPHY

Note: (There are a million bootleg tapes and albums as well as international and single releases which collectors might be interested in. Since what follows are only the official album and single releases I would recommend subscribing to an 'all Springsteen' magazine by the name of *Backstreets* for all that info and more. The address is: *Backstreets*, Box 51225, Seattle, WA 98115. For info and songs that were never released and everything you'd want to know about Bruce, the band and the inside story contact *Thunder Road* P.O. 171 Bogota N.J. 07603. All back issues are available.

# ALBUMS

## GREETINGS FROM ASBURY PARK, N.J.

Columbia KC 31903 (CBS 65480), 1973
Producers: Mike Appel and Jim Cretecos
Engineer: Louis Lahav
Personnel: Bruce Springsteen, Vincent 'Loper' Lopez, Clarence Clemmons (sic), Garry Tallent, David Sancious, Harold Wheeler, Richard Davis

Songs:
> Blinded By The Light   Growin' Up   Mary Queen Of Arkansas   Does This Bus Stop At 82nd Street?   Lost In The Flood   The Angel   For You   Spirit In The Night   It's Hard To Be A Saint In The City

## THE WILD, THE INNOCENT AND THE E STREET SHUFFLE

Columbia KC 32432 (CBS 65780), 1973
Producers: Mike Appel and Jim Cretecos
Engineer: Louis Lahav
Personnel: Vini 'Mad Dog' Lopez, Garry W. Tallent, Danny Federici, Clarence 'Nick' Clemons, David L. Sancious, Bruce Springsteen, Richard Blackwell, Albany 'Al' Tellone (From Newark N.J.)

Songs:
> The E Street Shuffle   4th Of July, Asbury Park (Sandy) Kitty's Back   Wild Billy's Circus Story   Incident On 57th Street   Rosalita (Come Out Tonight)   New York City Serenade

## BORN TO RUN

Columbia PC 33795 (CBS 69170), 1975
Producers: Bruce Springsteen, Jon Landau and Mike Appel
Engineer: Jimmy Iovine
Personnel: Bruce Springsteen, Garry Tallent, Ernest 'Boom'
Carter, Max M. Weinberg, David Sancious, Roy Bittan,
Clarence Clemons, Mike Appel, Steve Van Zandt, Randy
Brecker, Michael Brecker, David Sanborn, Wayne Andre,
Danny Federici, Suki Lahav, Richard Davis

Songs:

> *Thunder Road   Tenth Avenue Freeze-Out   Night
> Backstreets   Born To Run   She's The One   Meeting
> Across The River   Jungleland*

## DARKNESS ON THE EDGE OF TOWN

Columbia JC 35318 (CBS 86061), 1978
Producers: Jon Landau, Bruce Springsteen (assisted by Chuck
Plotkin)
Engineer: Jimmy Iovine
Personnel: Bruce Springsteen, Steve Van Zandt, Garry
Tallent, Danny Federici, Roy Bittan, Clarence Clemons, Max
Weinberg

Songs:

> *Badlands   Adam Raised A Cain   Something In The
> Night   Candy's Room   Racing In The Street   The
> Promised Land   Factory   Streets Of Fire   Prove It All
> Night   Darkness On The Edge Of Town*

*Also issued on picture disc*

## THE RIVER

Columbia PC2 36854, 1980
Producers: Bruce Springsteen, Jon Landau, Steve Van Zandt
(assisted by Chuck Plotkin)
   Engineers: Neil Dorfsman, Jimmy Iovine and Bob
Clearmountain
   Personnel: Roy Bittan, Clarence Clemons, Danny Federici,
Bruce Springsteen, Garry Tallent, Steve Van Zandt, Max
Weinberg. Guest appearance by Mark Volman and Howard
Kaylan (Flo and Eddie)

Songs:

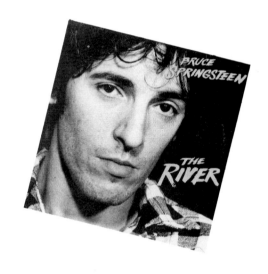

*The Ties That Bind   Sherry Darling   Jackson Cage   Two
Hearts   Independence Day   Hungry Heart   Out In The
Street   Crush On You   You Can Look (But You Better
Not Touch)   I Wanna Marry You   The River   Point
Blank   Cadillac Ranch   I'm A Rocker   Fade Away
Stolen Car   Ramrod   The Price You Pay   Drive All
Night   Wreck On The Highway*

## BRUCE SPRINGSTEEN AS REQUESTED
## AROUND THE WORLD

Columbia AS978 (PROMO ONLY)

Songs:

*Sherry Darling   The River   Cadillac Ranch   Hungry
Heart   Out In The Street   Born To Run   Badlands   Prove
It All Night   Rosalita (Come Out Tonight)*

## NEBRASKA

Columbia TC 38358 (CBS 85669), 1982
Producer: Bruce Springsteen
Engineer: Mike Batlin
Personnel: Bruce Springsteen

Songs:

*Nebraska   Atlantic City   Mansion On The Hill   Johnny
99   Highway Patrolman   State Trooper   Used Cars
Open All Night   My Father's House   Reason To Believe*

## BORN IN THE U.S.A.

Columbia QC 38653 (CBS 86304), 1984
Producers: Bruce Springsteen, Jon Landau, Chuck Plotkin,
Steve Van Zandt
Engineers: Toby Scott, Bob Clearmountain, Bill Scheniman
Personnel: Roy Bittan, Clarence Clemons, Danny Federici,
Garry Tallent, Steve Van Zandt, Bruce Springsteen, Max
Weinberg. Guest appearances by La Bamba and Ruth
Jackson

Songs:

*Born In The U.S.A.   Cover Me   Darlington County
Working On The Highway   Downbound Train   I'm On
Fire   No Surrender   Bobby Jean   I'm Goin' Down   Glory
Days   Dancing In The Dark   My Hometown*

## BRUCE SPRINGSTEEN BOX SET

INC. ASBURY PARK/THE WILD THE INNOCENT AND THE E
STREET SHUFFLE/BORN TO RUN

# 1972

BLINDED BY THE LIGHT/
AVENGING ANNIE
             Col - PLAYBACK 45 (PROMO)

# 1973

BLINDED BY THE LIGHT/
BLINDED BY THE LIGHT
             Col 4-45805 (PROMO)
BLINDED BY THE LIGHT/
THE ANGEL          Col 4-45805
SPIRIT IN THE NIGHT/
SPIRIT IN THE NIGHT    Col 4-45864 (PROMO)
SPIRIT IN THE NIGHT/
FOR YOU           Col 4 45864

# 1975

BORN TO RUN/
BORN TO RUN      Col 3 10209 (PROMO)
BORN TO RUN/
MEETING ACROSS THE RIVER
             Col 3 10209 (CBS 3840)
TENTH AVENUE FREEZE OUT/
TENTH AVENUE FREEZE OUT
             Col 3 10274 (PROMO)
TENTH AVENUE FREEZE OUT/
SHE'S THE ONE     Col 3 10274 (PROMO)

# 1978

PROVE IT ALL NIGHT/
PROVE IT ALL NIGHT    Col 10763 (PROMO)
PROVE IT ALL NIGHT/
FACTORY        Col 10763 (CBS 6424)
BADLANDS/
BADLANDS      Col 3 10801 (PROMO)
BADLANDS/
STREETS OF FIRE   Col 3 10801 (CBS 6532)

# 1980

HUNGRY HEART/
HELD UP WITHOUT A GUN
             Col 11 11391 (CBS 9309)
FADE AWAY/BE TRUE/
HELD UP WITHOUT A GUN (12")
             Col AS 928 (PROMO)

# 1981

SHERRY DARLING/
BE TRUE           CBS 9568
SANTA CLAUS IS COMING TO TOWN/
SANTA CLAUS IS COMING
TO TOWN      Col AE7 1332 (PROMO)
FADE AWAY/
BE TRUE           Col 11 11431
THE RIVER/
INDEPENDENCE DAY     CBS A 1179
THE RIVER/
BORN TO RUN/
ROSALITA       (12")   CBS A 131179
CADILLAC RANCH/
WRÉCK ON THE HIGHWAY   CBS A 1557

# 1982

ATLANTIC CITY/
MANSION ON THE HILL    CBS A 2794
OPEN ALL NIGHT/
BIG DAY BACK        CBS A 2969

# 1984

DANCING IN THE DARK/
PINK CADILLAC    Col 38-04463 (CBS A 4436)
DANCING IN THE DARK (BLASTER MIX)/
DANCING IN THE DARK (RADIO)/
DANCING IN THE DARK (DUB MIX)
(12")            Col 44-05028
DANCING IN THE DARK
(EXTENDED VERSION)/
PINK CADILLAC (12")      TA 4436
DANCING IN THE DARK/
PINK CADILLAC/
(SHAPED CADILLAC PICTURE DISC)  WA 4436
COVER ME/
JERSEY GIRL (LIVE) Col 38 04561 (CBS A 4662)
COVER ME/
JERSEY GIRL (LIVE)
(BRUCE SHAPED PICTURE DISC) (5")  WA 4662
BORN IN THE USA/
SHUT OUT THE LIGHT     Col 38 04680
COVER ME (US 12")/
COVER ME           Col 44 05087
(UNDERCOVER MIX)/COVER ME
(DUB I)/COVER ME (RADIO)/COVER
ME (DUB II)

## COMPILATIONS ON WHICH BRUCE HAS APPEARED

*THE HEAVYWEIGHTS*    Columbia A25174
*NO NUKES*    Elektra/Asylum ML-801
*HITLINE '80*    Columbia A25-890
*IN HARMONY 2 6 81*    BFC 37641

## SPRINGSTEEN HAS GUESTED ON THE FOLLOWING:-

### GARY U.S. BONDS/DEDICATION

*JOSÉ BLON* — Support Vocals
*THIS LITTLE GIRL* — Support vocals/guitar/ + Backing Vocals

### CLARENCE CLEMONS/RESCUE

*SAVIN' UP* — Guitar

### GRAHAM PARKER/THE UP ESCALATOR

*ENDLESS NIGHT* — Support Vocals

### LOU REED/STREET HASSLE

Monologue on *STREET HASSLE*

### DONNA SUMMER/DONNA SUMMER

GUITAR ON *PROTECTION*

# PROTEUS ROCKS

## The Best Rock 'n' Roll Reading from Proteus

☐ **TOYAH**
An illustrated fan's eyeview much-liked by Toyah herself.
by Gaynor Evans
UK £1.95
US $3.95

☐ **REGGAE: DEEP ROOTS MUSIC**
The definitive history of reggae. A major TV tie-in.
by Howard Johnson and Jim Pines
UK £5.95
US $10.95

☐ **BOOKENDS**
The first full study of Simon and Garfunkel, their joint and solo careers.
by Patrick Humphries
UK £5.95
US $10.95

☐ **PRETENDERS**
The first full study of this powerful and turbulent band.
by Chris Salewicz
UK £3.95
US $7.95

☐ **LOU REED**
A definitive profile of this almost reclusive figure.
by Diana Clapton
UK £4.95
US $9.95.

☐ **JAMES LAST**
A fully illustrated study of this world phenomenon of popular music.
by Howard Elson
UK £4.95
US $9.95

☐ **RARE RECORDS**
A complete illustrated guide to wax trash and vinyl treasures.
by Tom Hibbert
UK £4.95
US $9.95

☐ **THE PERFECT COLLECTION**
The 200 greatest albums, the 100 greatest singles selected and discussed by leading rock journalists.
Edited by Tom Hibbert
UK £4.95
US $9.95

☐ **EARLY ROCKERS**
All the seminal figures of rock 'n' roll:
Berry, Little Richard, Jerry Lee, Presley et al.
by Howard Elson
UK £4.95
US $9.95

**KATE BUSH** ☐
Complete illustrated story of this unique artist.
by Paul Kerton
UK £3.95
US $7.95

**BLACK SABBATH** ☐
Heavy Metal Superstars.
by Chris Welch
UK £4.95
US $9.95

**A-Z OF ROCK GUITARISTS** ☐
First illustrated encyclopaedia of guitar greats.
by Chris Charlesworth
UK £5.95
US $10.95

**A-Z OF ROCK DRUMMERS** ☐
Over 300 great drummers in this companion to ROCK GUITARISTS.
by Harry Shapiro
UK £5.95
US $10.95

**CHUCK BERRY** ☐
The definitive biography of the original Mr Rock 'n' Roll.
by Krista Reese
UK £4.95
US $8.95

**A CASE OF MADNESS** ☐
A big illustrated guide for fans of this insane band.
by Mark Williams
UK only £1.95

**TALKING HEADS** ☐
The only illustrated book about one of the most innovative bands of the 70s and 80s.
by Krista Reese
UK £4.95
US $9.95

**DURAN DURAN** ☐
The best-selling illustrated biography.
UK £1.95
US $3.95

**A TOURIST'S GUIDE TO JAPAN** ☐
Beautifully illustrated study of Sylvian and his colleagues.
by Arthur A. Pitt.
UK £1.95
US $3.95

**ILLUSTRATED POP QUIZ** ☐
Over 400 impossible questions for pop geniuses only.
by Dafydd Rees and Barry Lazell
UK £2.95
US $5.95

*order form overleaf*